The Book of Enoch

CW01582633

The Book of Enoch

by R. H. Charles.

This translation was originally published in 1917.

All rights reserved. No part of this book may be reproduced or transmitted in any form or by any means, electronic or mechanical, including photocopying, recording, or any information storage and retrieval system, without written permission from the publisher.

This book is sold on the condition that it shall not be lent, resold, rented out, or distributed in any other way, either for commercial purposes or otherwise, without prior consent from the publisher, in any binding or cover other than that in which it is published, and without a similar condition being imposed on the subsequent purchaser, including this one.

Every effort has been made to ensure that the information contained in this book is accurate and up to date. However, neither the author nor the publisher assumes any responsibility for errors or omissions, nor for any damages resulting from the use of the information contained herein.

In this book, trademark names may appear. Instead of using a trademark symbol each time a trademark name is used, names are used editorially, with no intention of infringing upon the respective owner's trademark.

Copyright © 2023 by Victoria Vioque, Edition
Copyright © 2023 by Theresa Ruiz J. for Cover Creation.
Copyright ©1917 by R.H. Charles for translate.

INDEX

Original Preface

Scarcely any department of theological science has, in the last few decades, received such marked attention and cultivation as that branch for which the Germans have adopted the felicitous appellation *Neutestamentliche Zeitgeschichte,*—the study of the age of Christ in its political, social, and religious aspects. Observant readers will not have failed to detect that the tendency of modern evangelical theology is to transfer the centre of interest from the work of Christ to the person of Christ. Hand in hand, and in close connection with this general tendency, certain auxiliary branches have assumed an importance hitherto not attributed to them. When the person of Christ forms the cynosure of all eyes, his surroundings proportionally grow in interest and importance; and hence it is not surprising that so much acumen and learning have been employed in the truly fascinating study of the Palestine of Christ's day in all its relations. The central sun casts its rays of resplendent light on ever-day objects, and these become prominent in proportion as they reflect this light.

In more than one respect the Book of Enoch is an important factor in these investigations. Being one of the oldest specimens of apocalyptic literature; reflecting in its different parts the convictions, feelings, and longings of the people of God at different stages of their development; written in imitation of the spirit of the prophets, with religious purposes and spiritual objects; it can safely be said to be an invaluable aid to the understanding of the religious and moral atmosphere in which the Saviour lived. It does not belong merely to the curiosities of literature, but is a book of positive worth, and the source of much information to the patient investigator.

This will suffice as an apology for a new translation of Enoch. In the translation the object has been to render as literally as possible, even if thereby the English should become a little harsh. Of course the notes do not pretend to unravel all the mysteries in this most mysterious of books; but it is hoped they will be of some assistance in understanding these intricacies. Naturally, these and the Introduction are, in part, a compilation; but the thoughts of others have been used with judgment and discrimination, and the sources are indicated. In all questions the writer has been independent, as will be seen by the fact that he has frequently departed from beaten paths.

Much remains yet to be done before this book will be entirely understood. Both its connection in sentiment and expression with the Old Testament, as well as its influence on Talmudic and Rabbinical lore, especially the latter, must, to a great extent, be the work of future investigations. But even with the limited means at hand this book, which an inspired writer thought worthy of citation, will not be read by the Christian theologian and minister without deep interest.

In conclusion the translator desires to express his thanks to his friend Prof. Dr. Adolf Harnack, of Giessen, Germany, for kind words and deeds in connection with this work; and to Prof. Dr. Ezra Abbot for his interest and aid in its publication.

GEORGE H. SCHODDE.

Columbus, Ohio, Nov. 21, 1881.

Editors' Preface

This volume serves as a gateway to the ancient and mystical realms explored in the Book of Enoch, aiming to bridge the gap between scholarly pursuit and general interest. At its core, this series is designed to offer students and enthusiasts alike affordable, accessible, and concise editions of pivotal texts, with the hope of illuminating the path for detailed study under the guidance of knowledgeable instructors. Beyond the academic sphere, we endeavor to captivate the curiosity of those who, though not formally studying these texts, find themselves drawn to the profound questions and narratives they present. Our mission extends to simplifying the complex, making the profound teachings and enigmatic passages of the Book of Enoch more readily available to a broader audience. This endeavor is not just about providing text; it's about opening doorways to understanding the foundational aspects of early Christian thought and the broader religious and philosophical discourse of the time. The decision to limit commentary and annotations stems from a desire to maintain focus and accessibility, acknowledging that more comprehensive analyses are within reach for those seeking deeper engagement. We encourage readers to view this as a starting point, a spark that ignites the pursuit of wisdom contained in more expansive works. In choosing the texts for this series, we've been mindful to include not only those that are lesser-known and hard to find but also fresh translations of some texts traditionally acknowledged within the official Apocrypha. Each selection is accompanied by an introduction that sets the stage, providing context and inviting readers to explore these ancient writings with fresh eyes and an open mind.

As custodians of these timeless stories and teachings, our goal is to make the significant but often overlooked texts like the Book of Enoch not just accessible, but relatable to modern seekers of knowledge. Through faithful and scholarly translations, we aim to connect past and present, offering insights into the origins of faith that continue to shape spiritual understanding today.

INTRODUCTION

THE APOCALYPTIC LITERATURE

As the Book of Enoch is, in some respects, the most notable extant apocalyptic work outside the canonical Scriptures, it will not be inappropriate to offer a few remarks here on the Apocalyptic Literature generally. In writing about the books which belong to this literature, Prof. Burkitt says very pointedly that "they are the most characteristic survival of what I will venture to call, with all its narrowness and its incoherence, the heroic age of Jewish history, the age when the nation attempted to realize in action the part of the peculiar people of God. It ended in catastrophe, but the nation left two successors, the Christian Church and the Rabbinical Schools, each of which carried on some of the old national aims. And of the two it was the Christian Church that was most faithful to the ideas enshrined in the Apocalypses, and it did consider itself, not without some reason, the fulfilment of those ideas. What is wanted, therefore, in studying the Apocalypses is, above all, sympathy with the ideas that underlie them, and especially with the belief in the New Age. And those who believe that in Christianity a new Era really did dawn for us ought, I think, to have that sympathy. . . . We study the Apocalypses to learn how our spiritual ancestors hoped again that God would make all right in the end; and that we, their children, are here to-day studying them is an indication that their hope was not wholly unfounded." [1]

---

[1] *Jewish and Christian Apocalypses*, pp. 15, 16 (1913).

Hope is, indeed, the main underlying motive-power which prompted the writers of the Apocalypses. And this hope is the more intensive and ardent in that it shines forth from a background which is dark with despair; for the Apocalyptists despaired of the world in which they lived, a world in which the godly were of no account, while the wicked seemed too often triumphant and prosperous. With evil everywhere around, the Apocalyptists saw no hope for the world as it was; for such a world there was no remedy, only destruction; if the good were ever to triumph it must be in a new world. Despairing, therefore, of the world around them, the Apocalyptists centred their hope upon a world to come, where the righteous would come to their own and evil would find no place. It is this thought which underlies the opening words of the Book of Enoch: "The words of the blessing of Enoch, wherewith he blessed the elect and righteous, who will be living in the day of tribulation, when all the wicked and godless are to be removed." Nowhere in this book is the essence of this hope more beautifully expressed than in a short metrical piece in the first chapter:

"But with the righteous He will make peace, And will protect the elect, And mercy shall be upon them.

"And they shall all belong to God, And they shall all be prospered, And they shall all be blessed.

"And He will help them all,

And light shall appear unto them,

And He will make peace with them" (1 Enoch i. 8).

In all the books belonging to this literature which have come down to us this hope is expressed more or less vividly; nor is the dark background wanting. with prophecies of coming wrath. It will, therefore, be realized that the Apocalyptic Literature is almost wholly concerned with the future; it is true that again and again the Apocalyptist glances at the contemporary history of the world around him, to which many a cryptic reference is made--a fact which necessitates some knowledge of the history of this period (*circa* 200 B.C.-A.D. 100) for a full understanding of the books in question--but these references are only made with a view to comforting the oppressed and afflicted with the thought that even the most mighty of earthly powers are shortly to be overthrown by. the advent of the new and glorious era when every injustice and all the incongruities of life will be done away with. So that every reference to the present is merely a position taken up from which to point to the future. Now, since, as we have seen, the Apocalyptists despair of any bettering of the present world, and therefore contemplate its destruction as the preliminary of the new order of things, they look *away* from this world in their visions of the future; they conceive of other-worldly forces coming into play in the reconstitution of things, and of society generally; and since these *are* other-worldly forces the supernatural plays a great part in the Apocalyptic Literature. This supernatural colouring will often strike the reader of this literature as fantastic, and at times *bizarre*; but this should not be permitted to obscure the reality which often lies behind these weird shadows. Mental visions are not always easily expressed in words; the seer who in a vision has received a message in some fantastic guise necessarily has the impress upon his mind of what he has seen when giving his message; and when he describes his vision the picture he presents is, in the nature of the case, more fantastic to the ear of the hearer than to the eye of him who saw it. Allowance should be made for this; especially by us Westerns who are so lacking in the rich imaginativeness of the Oriental. Our love of literalness hinders the play of the imagination because we are so apt to "materialize" a mental picture presented by another. The Apocalypses were written by and for Orientals, and we cannot do justice to them unless we remember this; but it would be best if we could get into the Oriental mind and look at things from that point of view.

Another thing which the reader of the Apocalyptic Literature must be prepared for is the frequent inconsistency of thought to be found there, together with variableness of teaching often involving contradiction. The reason of this is not to be sought simply in the fact that in the Apocalypses the hand of more than one author is frequently to be discerned, a fact which would easily account for divergence of views in one and the same book-no, the chief reason is that, on the one hand. the minds of the Apocalyptists were saturated with the traditional thoughts and ideas of the Old Testament, and, on the, other, they were eagerly absorbing the newer conceptions which the spirit of the age had brought into being. This occasioned a continual conflict of thought in their minds; the endeavour to harmonize the old and the new would not always succeed, and in consequence there often resulted a compromise which was illogical and which presented contradictions. Inconsistency of teaching on certain points is, therefore, not surprising under the circumstances.

Again, to realize the significance of much that is found in these Apocalypses one has to reckon with a rigid predestinarianism which was characteristic of the Apocalyptists as a whole. They started with the absolute conviction that the whole course of the world, from beginning to end, both as regards its physical changes and also in all that concerns the history of nations, their growth and decline, and of every single individual, was in every respect predetermined by God Almighty before all time. This belief of the Apocalyptists is well illustrated in one of the later Apocalypses by these words:

"For He hath weighed the age in the balance,

And by number hath He numbered the seasons;

Neither will He move nor stir things,

Till the measure appointed be fulfilled." (ii. (iv.) Esdras iv. 36, 37.)

Thus "the times and periods of the course of the world's history have been predetermined by God. The numbers of the years have been exactly fixed. This was a fundamental postulate of the Apocalyptists, who devoted much of their energy to calculations, based upon a close study of prophecy, as to the exact period when history should reach its consummation . . . the underlying idea is predestinarian." [2] But all these things, according to the Apocalyptists, were divine secrets hidden from the beginning the world, but revealed to God-fearing men to whom was accorded the faculty of peering into the hidden things of God and of understanding them; upon these men was laid the privilege and duty of revealing the divine secrets to others, hence their name of Apocalyptists or "revealers." It was because the Apocalyptists believed so firmly in this power which they possessed of looking into the deep things of God that they claimed to be able to measure the significance of what had happened in the past and of what was happening in the present; and upon the basis of this knowledge they believed that they also had the power, given them by God, of foreseeing the march of future events; above all, of knowing when the end of the world would come, a consummation towards which the whole history of the world had been tending from the beginning.

In spite of all the mysticism, sometimes of a rather fantastic kind, and of the frequently supramundane vision with which the Apocalyptic Literature abounds, the Apocalyptists fully realized the need of practical religion; they were upholders, of the Law, the loyal observance of which they regard as a necessity for all God-fearing men. In this the Apocalyptists were at one, in principle, with Pharisaism; but their conception of what constituted loyal observance of the Law differed from that of the Pharisees, for, unlike these, the Apocalyptists laid all stress on

---

[2] G. H. Box, *The Ezra Apocalypse*, pp. 35, 36 (1912).

the spirit of its observance rather than upon the letter. Characteristic of their attitude here are the words in 1 Enoch v. 4:

"But ye--ye have not been steadfast, nor done the commandments of the Lord,

But ye have turned away, and have spoken proud and hard words

With your impure mouths against His greatness, O ye hard-hearted, ye shall find no peace." And again, in xcix. 2:

"Woe to them that pervert the words of uprightness, And transgress the eternal Law."

We do not find in this Literature that insistence on the literal carrying-out of the minutest precepts of the Law which was characteristic of Pharisaism. Veneration for the Law is wholehearted; it is the real guide of life; punishment awaits those who ignore its guidance; but the Pharisaic interpretation of the Law and its requirements is alien to the spirit of the Apocalyptists.

As a whole, the Apocalyptic Literature presents an universalistic attitude very different from the nationalistic narrowness of the Pharisees. It is true, the Apocalyptists are not always consistent in this, but normally they embrace the Gentiles equally with the men of their own nation in the divine scheme of salvation; and, in the same way, the wicked who are excluded are not restricted to the Gentiles, but the Jews equally with them shall suffer torment hereafter according to their deserts.[3]

The Apocalyptic Literature, as distinct from the Apocalyptic Movement owing to which it took its rise, began to come into existence about the period 200-150 B.C.; at any rate, the earliest extant example of this

---

[3] The general Pharisaic point of view regarding this may be gathered from Matt. iii. 7-10.

Literature--the earliest portions of the Book of Enoch--belongs to this period. Works of an Apocalyptic character, continued to be written for about three centuries; the Second (Fourth) Book of Esdras, one of the most remarkable Apocalypses, belongs to the end of the first Christian century, approximately. There are Apocalypses of later date, some of subordinate interest are of much later date; but the real period of the Apocalyptic Literature is from about 200 B.C. to about A.D. 100; its beginnings date, therefore, from a time prior to that great landmark in Jewish history, the Maccabæan Era.

THE BOOK OF ENOCH: ITS COMPONENT PARTS AND THEIR DATES

The Book of Enoch is now usually designated 1 Enoch, to distinguish it from the later Apocalypse, *The Secrets of Enoch*, known as 2 Enoch. The former is also called the Ethiopic Enoch, the latter the Slavonic Enoch, after the languages of the earliest versions extant of each respectively. No manuscript of the original language of either is known to be in existence.

According to Canon Charles, the various elements of which our book in its present form is made up belong to different dates. The following table will show the dates of the different parts of the book. Canon Charles believes that these are approximately correct, without committing himself to the certainty of this in each case:

CHAPTERS xii.-xxxvi. xclii. xci. 12-17

"The Apocalypse of Weeks." The oldest pre-Maccabæan portions.

CHAPTERS vi.-xi. liv. 7-lv. 2 lx. lxv.-lxix. 25 cvi., cvii. Fragments of "The Book of Noah." Pre-Maccabæan at the latest.

CHAPTERS lxxxiii.-xc.

"The Dream-Visions," 165-161 B.C.

CHAPTERS lxxii.-lxxxii.

"The Book of the Heavenly Luminaries." Before 110 B.C.

CHAPTERS xxxvii.-lxxi. xci. 1-11, 18, 19-civ.

"The Parables," or "Similitudes." circa 105-64 B.C.

CHAPTERS i.-v.

The latest portion, but pre-Christian.

Chapter cv,

which consists of only two verses, cannot be dated; while cviii. is in the nature of an appendix, probably added subsequently, to the whole work.

While these dates may be regarded as approximately correct, it should be pointed out that differences of opinion exist among scholars on the subject. Schürer holds, for example, that, with the exception of chapters xxxvii.-lxxi. (the "Parables," or "Similitudes"), the entire book belongs to the period 130-100 B.C.; the "Parables" he assigns to a time not earlier than Herod the Great. Beer thinks that the "Dream-Visions" (chapters lxxxiii.-xc.) belong to the time of John Hyrcanus (135-105 B.C.), and he includes under the pre-Maccabæan portions only xci. 12-17, xcii. xciii. 1-14; and holds that the rest of the book was written before 64 B.C. Dalman maintains that it cannot be proved that the important section xxxvii.-lxxi. (the "Similitudes") is "the product of the pre-Christian period," though he fully recognizes its Jewish character. Burkitt regards the writer as "almost contemporary" with the philosopher Posidonius (135-51 B.C.). There is thus some diversity of opinion as to the date of the book among leading authorities. That it is, as a whole, pre-Christian, may be regarded as definitely established. More difficult is the question whether any portions of it are pre-Maccabæan; Charles gives various reasons for his belief that considerable parts are pre-Maccabæan; we are inclined to agree with him, though it may be questioned whether the last word on the subject has been spoken.

AUTHORSHIP

As the various parts of the book [4] clearly belong to different dates, diversity of authorship is what one is naturally led to expect; and of this there can, indeed, be no shadow of doubt. The author of the earliest portions was a Jew who lived, as Burkitt has shown, in northern Palestine, in the land of Dan, south-west of the Hermon range, near the headwaters of the Jordan. This is important, as it tends to show that the book, or books, is really Palestinian, and one which, therefore, circulated among Jews in Palestine. "If, moreover, the author came from the north, that helps to explain the influence the book had upon the Religion that was cradled in Galilee."[5] Of the authors of the other three books of which "Enoch" is made up (viz. "The Dream-Visions," "The Book of the Heavenly Luminaries," and "The Similitudes") we know nothing save what can be gathered from their writings as to their religious standpoint.

Charles holds that though there is not unity of authorship there is, none the less, uniformity; for, according to him, all the books were written by *Chassidim*, [5] or by their successors, the Pharisees. This contention has been strongly assailed and much weakened by Leszynsky in a recent work on the Sadducees. [7] While frankly recognizing the composite character of

---

[4] Burkitt rightly insists that we should speak of the collection as the books. not the book, of Enoch. [5] Burkitt, op. cit., 28-30.

[5] *i.e.* the " Pious ones." or " Saints." 7 *Die Saddurder* (1912).

the book, Leszynsky holds that the original portions of it [6] emanate from Sadducæan circles; and that the special object of the book originally was the bringing about of a reform of the calendar. He points to the ascription of the book to Enoch as supporting his contention, for Enoch lived 365 years, [7] *i.e.* is years correspond to the number of days in the solar year; the basis of reckoning time was one of the fundamental points of difference between the Pharisees and Sadducees, for whereas the former reckoned time by the lunar year (360 days), the latter did so by the solar year. Here a significant remark of Burkitt's is worth recalling; in writing about the false titles given to all the Apocalyptic books, he says: "There is another aspect of pseudonymous authorship to which I venture to think sufficient attention has not been given. It is this, that the names were not chosen out of mere caprice; they indicated to a certain extent what subjects would be treated and the point of view of the writer." [8] Further, the fact that "Enoch walked with God; and he was not; for God took him," [11] *i.e.* that he ascended into the heavens, is also significant; for he would thereby be just the one to know all about the heavenly luminaries; he was just the most appropriate author of a book which was to deal with astronomical questions. "The Sadducæan character of the original work," says Leszynsky, "is seen most clearly in the discussion regarding the calendar; chapters lxxii.lxxxii. are rightly called the Book of Astronomy: [9] 'the book of the courses of the luminaries of the heaven, the relations of each, according to their classes, their dominion and their seasons, according to their names and places of origin, and according to their months . . . with regard to all the years of the world and unto eternity, till

---

[6] i.e., according to him, i.-xxxvi., lxxii.-lxxxii., lxxxiii.-xc., xci. 12-17, xciii.

[7] See Gen. v. 21-23.

cit., p. 18. [11] Gen. v. 24.

[9] *i.e.* "The Book of the Heavenly Luminaries." as Charles calls it.

the new creation is accomplished which endureth till all eternity' (lxxii. 1). That sounds almost as though the author of the Book of jubilees had written it. That it is not a merely scientific interest which impels the writer to give expression to his astronomical theories may be seen from the words at the conclusion of the section: 'Blessed are all the righteous, blessed are all those who walk in the way of righteousness, and sin not as the sinners in the reckoning of all their days, in which the sun traverseth the heaven, entering into and departing from the portals for thirty days . . .' (lxxxii. 4-7). Herein one can discern quite clearly the tendency of the writer. He desires the adoption of the solar year, while his contemporaries wrongly followed a different reckoning, and therefore celebrated the feasts at the wrong time. The 'sinners who sin in the reckoning of the year' are the Pharisees; and the righteous ones who are blessed, the *Zaddîkim*, [10] who walk upon the paths of righteousness (*Zedek*) as the name is made to imply, are the Sadducees." [11] The point may appear small to us, but we may compare with it the Quartodeciman controversy in the Church during the second century. It is, at any rate, a strong point in favour of the Sadducæan authorship of "The Book of the Heavenly Luminaries."

The pre-Maccabæan portions (assuming that some portions of it are pre-Maccabæan) of the book of Enoch must certainly be ascribed to the *Chassidim*; but it is not on that account necessary to ascribe *all* the later portions to the Pharisees. Three points especially militate against this: some of the teaching concerning the Messiah; the, generally speaking, universalistic spirit, which is quite un-Pharisaic, and the attitude towards the Law, which is not that of the Pharisees. It is not to be denied that some portions (*e.g.* cii. 6 ff.) are from the hands of Pharisees; nor can it be doubted that the whole collection in its present form has been worked

---

[10] *i.e.* "the righteous"; a play on the word *Zaddûkîm*, the "sons of Zadok," *i.e.* the Sadducees.

over by a Pharisee, or Pharisees; but that all the post-Maccabæan portions in their original form emanated from Pharisaic circles does not appear to have been proved. It seems more likely that, with the exceptions already referred to, the various component parts of the book were written by Apocalyptists who belonged neither to Pharisaic nor yet to Sadducæan circles.

LANGUAGE

The Book of Enoch exists only in the Ethiopic Version; this was translated from the Greek Version, of which only a few portions are extant. [12] The Latin Version, which was also made from the Greek, is not extant, with the exception of i. 9, and cvi. 1-18; the fragment containing these two passages was discovered by the Rev. Al. R. James, of King's College, Cambridge, in the British Museum. The book was originally written either in Hebrew or Aramaic; Charles thinks that chapters vi.-xxxvi., lxxxiii.-xc. were Aramaic, the rest Hebrew. It is, however, very difficult to say for certain which of these two languages was really the original, because, as Burkitt says, "most of the most convincing proofs that the Greek text of Enoch is a translation from a Semitic language fit equally well with a Hebrew or an Aramaic original"; his opinion is that Aramaic was the

---

[11] Leszynsky, *op cit.*, pp. 253 ff.

[12] Chaps. i.-xxxii. 6. and xix. 3-xxi. 9 in a duplicate form were discovered at Akhmîm in 1886-1887; vi.-x. 14. xv. 8-xvi. x, and viii. 4-ix. 4 in a duplicate form, have been preserved in Syncellus; lxxxix. 42-49 occurs in a Greek Vatican MS. (No. 1809); there are also a few quotations in early Greek ecclesiastical writings; and i. 9, v.
4. xxvii. 2 are quoted in the Epistle of St. Jude 14, 15.

original language, "but that a few passages do seem to suggest a Hebrew origin, yet not decisively." [13]

GENERAL CONTENTS

The reader who comes to peruse the Book of Enoch for the first time will find much that appears to him strange and unattractive; he must not, however, be repelled by this; for in due time he will come to other arts of the book which he will soon see to be of real value from many points of view. But even regarding the less attractive parts, he will find that when these are carefully studied they contain more that is of interest than appears upon the surface. Unfortunately, the opening portion (i.-xxxvi.), which is naturally read first, contains a good deal of the least important parts of the whole book; some passages are even repellent. It is well to remember the point, already referred to, that there are at least four quite independent books included in the "Book of Enoch," exclusive of certain "Noah" fragments and other pieces (see below); the student is, therefore, advised to treat these as separate works, and to read them as such. There is no reason to begin with the book which happens to come first, especially as the first thirty-six chapters do not all belong together. 16F14 But, in any case, it will be found most useful to have some general idea of the contents of each of the different books before beginning to read them. For this purpose a brief *résumé* of each is given here.

i. *The Book of Enoch* (chapters xii.-xxxvi.). The book begins With a Dream-Vision of Enoch. In this dream Enoch is asked to intercede for the watchers of heaven, *i.e.* the angels, who had left their heavenly home to

---

[13] *Op. cit.*, p. 27.

[14] It is a great pity that one system of chapter-enumeration runs through the whole volume; if each separate book began with chap. i. it would be much better. For obvious reasons this cannot be done here; see Editors' General Preface.

commit iniquity with the daughters of men. He writes out the petition (cp. the title "Enoch the Scribe") the fallen angels make, and then retires to await the answer, which comes to him in a series of visions. These visions are not quite easy to follow; they are evidently incomplete and somewhat confused; in all probability the text has suffered in transmission. At any rate, the petition is refused; Enoch declares to the fallen angels the doom which, as he has been taught in the visions, is to be their lot; the final words of the message which he is bidden to give them are: "You have no peace" (xii.-xvi.). There follow then accounts of the different journeys which Enoch makes, being conducted by angels of light, through certain parts of the earth, and through Sheol. After the account of the *first journey* (xvii.-xix.) a short enumeration is made of the archangels, seven in number, and their functions (xx.). In the *second journey* is described the place of final punishment of the fallen angels: "This place is the prison of the angels and here they will imprisoned for ever." From thence Enoch is taken to Sheol; then to the west, where he sees the luminaries of heaven. After that the angels show him "seven magnificent mountains," upon one of which is the throne of God; he sees also the Tree of Life, which is to be given to the holy and. righteous after the great judgement. From thence he comes back to the centre of the earth and sees the "blessed place," Jerusalem, and the "accursed valley" (xxi.-xxvii.). The book concludes with what appear to be fragments of other journeys, to the east, to the north, and to the south. Of special interest here is the mention of the Garden of Righteousness, and the Tree of Wisdom (xxviii.-xxxvi.).

Much that is written in these chapters may appear pointless and uninspiring; but we must bear in mind the purpose that lies behind it all. The fallen angels were believed to have brought sin on to the earth; all the wickedness of the world the Apocalyptist traces back to them. This cause of sin must be wholly destroyed before righteousness can come truly to its own. Therefore the Apocalyptist has a practical aim in view when describing in much detail the final place of punishment of the fallen angels; for here, too, are to come all those who by sin are the offspring of this race. No less does he delight in telling of the abode of joy prepared for the righteous. That all these descriptions were constructed out of the imagination of the Apocalyptist, based largely, no doubt, upon popular tradition, did not detract from their practical value for the people of his day. He was a preacher of righteousness who looked forward in absolute conviction to the final overthrow of sin; and all his visions have as their motive-power the yearning for and belief in the triumph of righteousness over sin. One of a like mind wrote later on, in a kind of preface to his book, these significant words, which sum up the essence of the teaching of this book:

And destroy all the spirits of the reprobate, and the children of the Watchers. because they have wronged mankind. Destroy all wrong from the face of the earth, and let every evil work come to an end: and let the plant of righteousness and truth appear: and it shall prove a blessing: the works of righteousness and truth shall be planted in truth and joy for evermore.

ii. *The Parables* (chapters xxxvii.-lxxi.). There are three Parables. or Similitudes, and they all have as their underlying thought the destruction of evil and the triumph of righteousness, as in the preceding book. But here some new and important elements are introduced which give special value to this book.

The *first parable* (xxxviii.-xliv.) is a prophecy of coming judgement upon the wicked, and especially the kings and mighty ones on the earth. On the other hand, the Apocalyptist sees in his vision the abode and resting-places of the righteous who are continually praising the "Lord of Spirits "; this is the usual title given -to God in this book. Here occurs the first mention of the "Elect One" (cp. Luke xxiii. 35). In the presence of the Lord of Spirits are also the four Archangels and innumerable companies of other angels. Here he learns many secrets of the heavens; a fragment on Wisdom (xlii.), which recalls some passages in Ecclus. xxiv., comes in the middle of the secrets, and is clearly out of place. The *second parable* (xlv.-lvii.) continues the same theme and further develops it. Of special importance is the sitting of the Elect One on the throne of glory as Judge (xlv. 3), and the mention of His title, "Son of Man" (xlvi. 2). The thought of the vindication of the righteous is marred by their joy at vengeance upon the wicked. A particularly striking passage is chapter xlviii. 1-7, which speaks of the inexhaustible fountain of righteousness reserved for the holy and elect in the presence of the Son of Man and of the Lord of Spirits. The Apocalyptist prophesies further of the repentance of the Gentiles (chapter l.), an universalistic note of significance, and speaks of the Resurrection of the dead in a notable passage:

And In those days shall the earth also give back that which has been entrusted to it, And Sheol also shall give back that which it has received, And Hell shall give back that which it owes.

The parable ends with an account of the judgement, followed by two short passages on the last struggle of the heathen powers against Israel (lvi. 5-8), and the return from the Dispersion (lvii.), which do not appear to be in their original place. The *third parable* (lviii.-lxxi.) has clearly suffered largely from the intrusion of alien matter, and is probably incomplete. Its main theme is the final judgement upon all flesh, and especially upon the great ones of -the earth; the judge is the Son of Man. Some of the passages which speak of the future reward of the righteous are full of beauty; the following is well worth quoting:

And the righteous and elect shall have risen from the earth, And ceased to be of downcast countenance.

And they shall have been clothed with garments of glory.

And they shall be garments of life from the Lord of Spirits: And your garments shall not grow old.

Nor your glory pass away before the Lord of Spirits.

A large Noah fragment comes in the middle of the Parable (see p. xxvi below). The close of this Parable is contained in lxix. 26-29; the account of Enoch's final translation (lxx.), and two of Enoch's visions (lxxi.) are out of place.

iii. *The Book of the Courses of the Heavenly Luminaries* (chapters lxxii.-lxxxii.). In lxxiv. 12 it says: "And the sun and the stars bring in all the years exactly, so that they do not advance or delay their position by a single day unto eternity; but complete the years with perfect justice in 364 days." [15] This gives the key-note of this book, viz. that time is to be reckoned by the sun, not by the moon (see further on this the section on Authorship, above). Until we come to chapter lxxx. this book is uninteresting in the extreme; it purports to tell in detail of the laws by which the sun, moon, stars and the winds are governed; they are described by Uriel, "the holy angel," to the Apocalyptist. The four quarters of the world, the seven mountains and the seven rivers are also dealt with. "The author has no other interest save a scientific one coloured by Jewish conceptions and beliefs." [16] It is, however, different when we come to chapter lxxx. 2-8; the whole tone alters in these verses, in which it is said that owing to the sin of men the moon and the sun will mislead them. An ethical thought is thus brought in which is wholly lacking in the previous chapters of this book; this is also true of chapter lxxxi.; it is probable that neither of these chapters stood here originally.

Regarding the point of the 364 days to the year which the writer of this book makes, Charles says that "he did this only through sheer incapacity for appreciating an thing better; for he must have been acquainted with the solar year of 365¼ days. His acquaintance with the Greek cycles shows this. . . . The author's reckoning of the year at 364 days may be partly due to his opposition to heathen systems, and partly to the fact that 364 is divisible by seven, and amounts to fifty-two weeks exactly." [17] In any case, he is opposed to the lunar year, the Pharisaic way of reckoning time; and this is an important point in favour of Sadducæan authorship. It will be noted that this book was written in post-Maccabæan times; it was after the Maccabæan struggle that the Sadducees and Pharisees appeared as parties definitely opposed to one another. [18]

---

[15] See also lxxxii. 4-6. it.

[16] Charles, *The Book of Enoch*, p. 147 (1912).

[17] *Op. cit.* p. 150.

[18] for the points of difference between the Pharisees and Sadducees see the present writer's *The Books of the Apocrypha, their Origin, Teaching, and Contents*, chap. vii. (1914).

iv. *The Dream-Visions* (chapters lxxxiii.-xc.). This book consists of two dream-visions; the first deals with the judgement brought upon the world by the deluge on account of sin; the origin of sin is again traced to the angels who fell. It concludes with a hymn of praise to God in which a prayer is offered that all flesh may not be destroyed (lxxxiii.-lxxxiv.). The second dream-vision is much longer; it gives in brief outline the history of the world to the founding of the Messianic Kingdom. First, the patriarchs, symbolized by bulls, etc. (lxxxv.); then the fallen angels, also described in symbolic language, and their punishment (lxxxvi.-lxxxviii.). The history then proceeds to deal more specifically with Israel from the time of Noah to the Maccabæan revolt (lxxxix.-xc. 19). Throughout the dream-vision symbolic language is used; the faithful in Israel are spoken of as the sheep, while the Gentiles are symbolized by wild beasts and birds of prey.

The dream-vision concludes with some familiar eschatological notes: the judgement and condemnation of the wicked; the establishment of the New Jerusalem; the conversion of the Gentiles, who become subject to Israel; the gathering-in of the dispersed Israelites; the resurrection of the righteous dead and the setting-up of the Messianic Kingdom on the appearance of the Messiah (xc. 20-38).

v. *The Concluding Section* of the Book (xcii.-cv.; xci. x-10, 18, 19 also belong here) is a complete, though short, work; but there are some obvious interpolations, and it is quite possible that some parts of the text are dislocated. This makes the understanding of the book difficult; but if we follow Charles's guidance here the difficulties will disappear. He says that this concluding piece has in some degree suffered at the hands the final editor of the book, both in the way of direct interpolation and of severe dislocations of the text. The interpolations are: xci. 11, xciii. 11-14, xciv. 7[d], xcvi. 2. The dislocations of the text are a more important feature of the book. They are confined (with the exception of xciii. 13-14, and of cvi. 17[a] which should be read immediately after cvi. 14) to xci.-xciii. All critics are agreed as to the chief of these. xci. 12-17 should undoubtedly be read directly after xciii. . . . Taken together xciii. 1-10, xci. 12-17 form an independent whole--the Apocalypse of Weeks-which has been incorporated in xci.-civ. . . . The remaining dislocations need only to be pointed out in order to be acknowledged. On other grounds we find that xci.-civ. is a book of different authorship from that of the rest of the sections. Now, this being so, this section obviously begins with xcii.: 'Written by Enoch the Scribe.' etc. On xcii. follows xci. 1-10, 18, 19 as a natural sequel, where Enoch summons his children to receive his parting words. Then comes the Apocalypse of weeks, xciii. 1-10, xci. 12-17. The original order of the text, therefore, was: xcii. xci. 1-10, 18, 19, xciii. 1-10, xci. 12-17. xciv. These dislocations were the work of the editor, who put the different books of Enoch together, and added lxxx. and lxxxi." [19]

This book is concerned with the question of the final reward of the righteous and the final punishment of the wicked. . But a new teaching of great importance is put forth here. Hitherto it had been taught that although much incongruity and apparent injustice were to be found on this earth owing to the suffering of the righteous and the prosperity of the wicked,.

nevertheless all things would be righted in the world to come, where the wicked would receive their deserts, and the righteous would come to their own. In this book it is taught that retribution will overtake the wicked, and the righteous will have peace and prosperity, even on this earth, with the setting-up of the Messianic Kingdom; and that at the last there will come, with the final judgement, the destruction of the former heaven and earth, and the creation of a new heaven. Then will follow the resurrection of the spirits of the righteous dead who will live for ever in peace and joy, while the wicked will perish everlastingly. The important point, which is a development, is the idea of the punishment of the wicked taking place on this earth, the very scene of their unrighteous triumphs.

vi. *The Noah Fragments* (vi.-xi, lvii. 7-lv. 2, ix. lxv.-lxix. 25, cvi., cvii.). These fragments are not of much importance; the main topics touched upon are the fall of the angels and sin among men in consequence; judgement on mankind, *i.e.* the Deluge, and the preservation of Noah.

---

[19] *Op. cit.*, p. 218.

The first five chapters are generally field to be as late as any part of the whole collection; they deal with the punishment hereafter of the wicked and the blessedness of the righteous.

Chapter cviii., which reads like a final word to the whole collection, touches upon the same theme.

THE IMPORTANCE OF THE BOOK FOR THE STUDY OF CHRISTIAN ORIGINS

This is a subject which cannot be thoroughly appreciated without studying the book in detail, especially from its doctrinal standpoint, and seeing in how many aspects it represents the doctrine and the popular conceptions of the Jews during the two last pre-Christian centuries. To do this here would involve a far too extended investigation; it must suffice to indicate a few of the many points which should be studied; from these it will be seen how important the book is for the study of Christian origins. Charles says that "the influence of 1 Enoch on the New Testament has been greater than that of all the other apocryphal and pseudepigraphical books put together"; and he gives a formidable list of passages in the New Testament which "either in phraseology or idea directly depend on, or are illustrative of, passages in 1 Enoch," as well as a further list showing that various doctrines in 1 Enoch had "an undoubted share in moulding the corresponding New Testament doctrines." These passages should be studied-and they will be found to be a most interesting study--in Charles's work already referred to several times, pp. xcv.-ciii.; and with these should be read the section on the Theology of the Book of Enoch, pp. ciii.-cx. Another book of great value and interest--also already quoted--is Burkitt's *Jewish and Christian Apocalypses*. In dealing with the subject of 1 Enoch and the Gospels, this writer points out that the former "contains a serious attempt to account for the presence of Evil in human history, and this attempt claims our attention, because it is in essentials the view presupposed in the Gospels, especially in the Synoptic Gospels. It is when you study Matthew, Mark, and Luke against the background of the Books of Enoch that you see them in their true perspective. In saying this I have no intention of detracting from the importance of what the, Gospels report to us. On the contrary, it puts familiar words into their proper setting. Indeed, it seems to me that some of the best-known Sayings of Jesus only appear in their true light if regarded as *Midrash* upon words and concepts that were familiar to those who heard the Prophet of Galilee, though now they have been forgotten by Jew and Christian alike" (p. 21). He then gives an illustration of this from Matt. xii. 43-45, Luke xi.

24--26. Of still greater interest are his remarks upon the relationship between 1 Enoch lxii. and Matt. xxv, 31-46; he believes that "the Similitudes of Enoch are presupposed in the scene from Matthew." The whole of the discussion which follows should be read.

The special points of interest that should be studied in seeking to realize the importance of these books of Enoch for the study of Christian origins are the problems of evil, including, of course, the subjects of dæmonology, and future judgement; the Messiah and the Messianic Kingdom--the title "Son of Man" is of special importance--and the Resurrection. There are, of course, other subjects which will suggest themselves in studying the book.

Abbreviations, brackets, and symbols specially used in the translation of enoch

E denotes the Ethiopic Version.

G^s denotes the fragments of the Greek Version preserved In Syncellus: in the case of $8^b 9^b$ there are two forms of the text, G^{s1} G^{s2}.

G^g denotes the large fragment of the Greek Version discovered at Akhmîm, and deposited in the Gizeh Museum, Cairo.

The following brackets are used in the translation of 1 Enoch:

⌈ ⌉. The use of these brackets means that the words so enclosed are found in G^g but not In E.

⌈⌈ ⌉⌉. The use of these brackets means that the words so enclosed are found in E but not in G^g or G^s.

⟨ ⟩ . The use of these brackets means that the words so enclosed are restored.

[ ] The use of these brackets means that the words so enclosed are interpolations.

( ). The use of these brackets means that the words so enclosed are supplied by the editor.

The use of **thick type** denotes that the words so printed are emended.

† † corruption in the text.

. . . = some words which have been lost.

The Book Of Enoch

SECTION I. CHAPTERS 1-36

CHAPTER I.

1. The words of the blessing of Enoch, wherewith he blessed the elect [[and]] righteous, who will be living in the day of tribulation, when all the wicked [[and godless]] are to be removed.

2. And he took up his parable and said--Enoch a righteous man, whose eyes were opened by God, saw the vision of the Holy One in the heavens, [which] the angels showed me, and from them I heard everything, and from them I understood as I saw, but not for this generation, but for a remote one which is for to come.

3. Concerning the elect I said, and took up my parable concerning them: The Holy Great One will come forth from His dwelling,

4. And the eternal God will tread upon the earth, (even) on Mount Sinai,

[And appear from His camp]

And appear in the strength of His might from the heaven of heavens.

5. And all shall be smitten with fear

And the Watchers shall quake,

And great fear and trembling shall seize them unto the ends of the earth.

6. And the high mountains shall be shaken,

And the high hills shall be made low,

And shall melt like wax before the flame

7. And the earth shall be [wholly] rent in sunder, And all that is upon the earth shall perish, And there shall be a judgement upon all (men).

8. But with the righteous He will make peace. And will protect the elect, And mercy shall be upon them. And they shall all belong to God, And they shall be prospered, And they shall [all] be blessed. [And He will help them all], And light shall appear unto them, [And He will make peace with them].

9. And behold! He cometh with ten thousands of [His] holy ones To execute judgement upon all, And to destroy [all] the ungodly: And to convict all flesh Of all the works [of their ungodliness] which they have ungodly committed, And of all the hard things which ungodly sinners [have spoken] against Him.

CHAPTER II.

1. Observe ye everything that takes place in the heaven, how they do not change their orbits, [and] the luminaries which are in the heaven, how they all rise and set in order each in its season, and transgress not against their appointed order.

2. Behold ye the earth, and give heed to the things which take place upon it from first to last, [how **steadfast** they are], how [none of the things upon earth] change, [but] all the works of God appear [to you].

3. Behold the summer and the winter, [[how the whole earth is filled with water, and clouds and dew and rain lie upon it]].

CHAPTER III.

Observe and see how (in the winter) all the trees [[seem as though they had withered and shed all their leaves, except fourteen trees, which do not lose their foliage but retain the old foliage from two to three years till the new comes.

CHAPTER IV.

And again, observe ye the days of summer how the sun is above the earth over against it. And you seek shade and shelter by reason of the heat of the sun, and the earth also burns with growing heat, and so you cannot tread on the earth, or on a rock by reason of its heat.

CHAPTER V.

1. Observe [[ye]] how the trees cover themselves with green leaves and bear fruit: wherefore give ye heed [and know] with regard to all [His works], and recognize how He that liveth for ever hath made them so.

2. And [all] His works go on [thus] from year to year for ever, and all the tasks [which] they accomplish for Him, and [their tasks] change not, but according as [[God]] hath ordained so is it done.

3. And behold how the sea and the rivers in like manner accomplish and [change not] their tasks [from His commandments].

4. But ye--ye have not been steadfast, nor done the commandments of the Lord, But ye have turned away and spoken proud and hard words With your impure mouths against His greatness. Oh, ye hard-hearted, ye shall find no peace.

5. Therefore shall ye execrate your days,

And the years of your life shall perish,

And [the years of your destruction] shall be multiplied in eternal execration, And ye shall find no mercy.

6*a*. In those days ye shall make your names an eternal execration unto all the righteous, *b*. And by you shall [all] who curse, curse,

And all the sinners [and godless] shall
imprecate by you, 7*c*. And for you the
godless there shall be a curse.

6*d*. And all the . . . shall rejoice,

e. And there shall be forgiveness of sins,

f. And every mercy and peace and forbearance:

g. There shall be salvation unto them, a goodly light.

i. And for all of you sinners there
shall be no salvation, *j* But on you
all shall abide a curse.

7*a*. But for the elect there shall be
light and joy and peace, *b*. And they
shall inherit the earth.

8 And then there shall be bestowed upon the elect wisdom, And they shall all live and never again sin, Either through ungodliness or through pride: But they who are wise shall be humble.

9 And they shall not again transgress,

Nor shall they sin all the days of their life,

Nor shall they die of (the divine) anger or wrath,

But they shall complete the number of the days of their life.

And their lives shall be increased in peace,

And the years of their joy shall be multiplied, In eternal gladness and peace, All the days of their life.

CHAPTER VI.

1. And it came to pass when the children of men had multiplied that in those days were born unto them beautiful and comely daughters. 2. And the angels, the children of the heaven, saw and lusted after them, and said to one another: 'Come, let us choose us wives from among the children of men and beget us children.' 3. And Semjâzâ, who was their leader, said unto them: 'I fear ye will not indeed agree to do this deed, and I alone shall have to pay the penalty of a great sin.' 4. And they all answered him and said: 'Let us all swear an oath, and all bind ourselves by mutual imprecations not to abandon this plan but to do this thing.' 5. Then sware they all together and bound themselves by mutual imprecations upon it. 6. And they were in all two hundred; who descended [in the days] of **Jared** on the summit of Mount Hermon, and they called it Mount Hermon, because they had sworn and bound themselves by mutual imprecations upon it. 7. And these are the names of their leaders: Sêmîazâz, their leader, Arâkîba, Râmêêl, Kôkabîêl, Tâmîêl, Râmîêl, Dânêl, Êzêqêêl, Barâqîjâl, Asâêl, Armârôs, Batârêl, Anânêl, Zaqîêl, Samsâpêêl, Satarêl, Tûrêl, Jômjâêl, Sariêl. 8. These are their chiefs of tens.

CHAPTER VII.

1. And all the others together with them took unto themselves wives, and each chose for himself one, and they began to go in unto them and to defile themselves with them, and they taught them charms and enchantments, and the cutting of roots, and made them acquainted with plants. 2. And they became pregnant, and they bare great giants, whose height was three thousand ells: 3. Who consumed all the acquisitions of men. And when men could no longer sustain them, 4. the giants turned against them and devoured mankind. 5. And they began to sin against birds, and beasts, and reptiles, and fish, and to devour one another's

flesh, and drink the blood. 6. Then the earth laid accusation against the lawless ones.

CHAPTER VIII.

1. And Azâzêl taught men to make swords, and knives, and shields, and breastplates, and made known to them **the metals** ⟨of the earth⟩ and the art of working them, and bracelets, and ornaments, and the use of antimony, and the beautifying of the eyelids, and all kinds of costly stones, and all colouring tinctures. 2. And there arose much godlessness, and they committed fornication, and they were led astray, and became corrupt in all their ways. Semjâzâ taught enchantments, and root-cuttings, Armârôs the resolving of enchantments, Barâqîjâl, (taught) astrology, Kôkabêl the constellations, **Ezêqêêl the knowledge of the clouds**, ⟨Araqiêl the signs of the earth, Shamsiêl the signs of the sun⟩ , and Sariêl the course of the moon. And as men perished, they cried, and their cry went up to heaven . . .

CHAPTER IX.

1. And then Michael, Uriel, Raphael, and Gabriel looked down from heaven and saw much blood being shed upon the earth, and all lawlessness being wrought upon the earth. 2. And they said one to another: 'The earth made †without inhabitant cries the voice of their crying† up to the gates of heaven. 3 [[And now to you, the holy ones of heaven]], the souls of men make their suit, saying, "Bring our cause before the Most High.".' 4. And they said to the Lord **of the ages**: 'Lord of lords, God of gods, King of kings, ⟨and God of the ages⟩ , the throne of Thy glory (standeth) unto all the generations of the ages, and Thy name holy and glorious and blessed unto all the ages! 5. Thou hast made all things, and power over all things hast Thou: and all things are naked and open in Thy sight, and Thou seest all things, and nothing can hide itself

from Thee. 6. Thou seest what Azâzêl hath done, who hath taught all unrighteousness on earth and revealed the eternal secrets which were (preserved) in heaven, which men were striving to **learn**: 7. And Semjâzâ, to whom Thou hast given authority to bear rule over his associates. 8. And they have gone to the daughters of men upon the earth, and have slept with the women, and have defiled themselves, and revealed to them all kinds of sins. 9. And the women have borne giants, and the whole earth has thereby been filled with blood and unrighteousness. 10. And now, behold, the souls of those who have died are crying and making their suit to the gates of heaven, and their lamentations have ascended: and cannot **cease** because of the lawless deeds which are wrought on the earth. 11. And Thou knowest all things before they come to pass, and Thou seest these things and Thou dost suffer them, and Thou dost not say to us what we are to do to them in regard to these.'

CHAPTER X.

1. Then said the Most High, the Holy and Great One spake, and sent **Uriel** to the son of Lamech, and said to him: 2. ' ⟨Go to Noah⟩ and tell him in my name "Hide thyself!" and reveal to him the end that is approaching: that the whole earth will be destroyed, and a deluge is about to come upon the whole earth, and will destroy all that is on it. 3. And now instruct him that he may escape and his seed may be preserved for all the generations of the world.' 4. And again the Lord said to Raphael: 'Bind Azâzêl hand and foot, and cast him into the darkness: and make an opening in the desert, which is in Dûdâêl, and cast him therein. 5. And place upon him rough and jagged rocks, and cover him with darkness, and let him abide there for ever, and cover his face that he may not see light. 6. And on the day of the great judgement he shall be cast into the fire. And heal the earth which the angels have corrupted, and proclaim the healing of the earth, that they may heal the plague, and that all the children of men may not perish through all the secret things that the

Watchers have **disclosed** and have taught their sons. 8. And the whole earth has been corrupted through the works that were taught by Azâzêl: to him ascribe all sin.' 9. And to Gabriel said the Lord: 'Proceed against the bastards and the reprobates, and against the children of fornication: and destroy [the children of fornication and] the children of the Watchers from amongst men [and cause them to go forth]: send them one against the other that they may destroy each other in battle: for length of days shall they not have. 10. And no request that they *(i.e.* their fathers) make of thee shall be granted unto their fathers on their behalf; for they hope to live an eternal life, and that each one of them will live five hundred years.' 11. And the Lord said unto Michael: 'Go, **bind** Semjâzâ and his associates who have united themselves with women so as to have defiled themselves with them in all their uncleanness. 12. And when their sons have slain one another, and they have seen the destruction of their beloved ones, bind them fast for seventy generations in the **valleys** of the earth, till the day of their judgement and of their consummation, till the judgement that is for ever and ever is consummated. 13. In those days they shall be led off to the abyss of fire: ⟨and⟩ to the torment and the prison in which they shall be confined for ever. And whosoever shall be **condemned** and destroyed will from thenceforth be bound together with them to the end of all generations. 15. And destroy all the spirits of the reprobate and the children of the Watchers, because they have wronged mankind. Destroy all wrong from the face of the earth and let every evil work come to an end: and let the plant of righteousness and truth appear: [and it shall prove a blessing; the works of righteousness and truth] shall be planted in truth and joy for evermore.

17 And then shall all the righteous escape,

And shall live till they beget thousands of children,

And all the days of their youth
and their **old age** Shall they
complete in peace.

18 And then shall the whole earth be tilled in righteousness, and shall all be planted with trees and be full of blessing. 19. And all desirable trees shall be planted on it, and they shall plant vines on it: and the vine which they plant thereon shall yield wine in abundance, and as for all the seed which is sown thereon each measure (of it) shall bear a thousand, and each measure of olives shall yield ten presses of oil. 20. And cleanse thou the earth from all oppression, and from all unrighteousness, and from all sin, and from all godlessness: and all the uncleanness that is wrought upon the earth destroy from off the earth. 21. [And all the children of men shall become righteous], and all nations shall offer adoration and shall praise Me, and all shall worship Me. And the earth shall be cleansed from all defilement, and from all sin, and from all punishment, and from all torment, and I will never again send (them) upon it from generation to generation and for ever.

CHAPTER XI.

1. And in those days I will open the store chambers of blessing which are in the heaven, so as to send them down [upon the earth] over the work and labour of the children of men. 2. And truth and peace shall be associated together throughout all the days of the world and throughout all the generations **of men**.'

CHAPTER XII.

1. Before these things Enoch was hidden, and no one of the children of men knew where he was hidden, and where he abode, and what had become of him. 2. And his activities had to do with the Watchers, and his days were with the holy ones.

3. And I, Enoch was blessing the Lord of **majesty** and the King of the ages, and lo! the Watchers called me--Enoch the scribe--and said to me: 4.

'Enoch, thou scribe of righteousness, go, †declare† to the Watchers of the heaven who have left the high heaven, the holy eternal place, and have defiled themselves with women, and have done as the children of earth do, and have taken unto themselves wives: "Ye have wrought great destruction on the earth: 5. And ye shall have no peace nor forgiveness of sin: and inasmuch as †they† delight themselves in †their† children, 6. The murder of †their† beloved ones shall †they† see, and over the destruction of †their† children shall †they† lament, and shall make supplication unto eternity, but mercy and peace shall ye not attain."'

CHAPTER XIII.

1. And Enoch went and said: 'Azâzêl, thou shalt have no peace: a severe sentence has gone forth against thee to put thee in bonds: 2. And thou shalt not have toleration nor †request† granted to thee, because of the unrighteousness which thou hast taught, and because of all the works of godlessness and unrighteousness and sin which thou hast shown to men.' 3. Then I went and spoke to them all together, and they were all afraid, and fear and trembling seized them. 4. And they besought me to draw up a petition for them that they might find forgiveness, and to read their petition in the presence of the Lord of heaven. 5. For from thenceforward they could not speak (with Him) nor lift up their eyes to heaven for shame of their sins for which they had been condemned. 6. Then I wrote out their petition, and the prayer in regard to their spirits and their deeds individually and in regard to their requests that they should have forgiveness and length ⟨of days⟩ †. 7. And I went off and sat down at the waters of Dan, in the land of Dan, to the south of the west of Hermon: I read their petition till I fell asleep. 8. And behold a dream came to me, and visions fell down upon me, and I saw visions of chastisement, ⌊and a voice came bidding (me)⌋ I to tell it to the sons of heaven, and reprimand them. 9. And when I awaked, I came unto them, and they were all sitting gathered together, weeping in 'Abelsjâîl, which is between Lebanon and

Sênêsêr, with their faces covered. 10. And I recounted before them all the visions which I had seen in sleep, and I began to speak the words of righteousness, and to reprimand the heavenly Watchers.

CHAPTER XIV.

1. The book of the words of righteousness, and of the reprimand of the eternal Watchers in accordance with the command of the Holy Great One in that vision. 2. I saw in my sleep what I will now say with a tongue of flesh and with the breath of my mouth: which the Great One has given to men to converse therewith and understand with the heart. 3. As He has created and given [[to man the power of understanding the word of wisdom, so hath He created me also and given]] me the power of reprimanding the Watchers, the children of heaven. 4. I wrote out your petition, and in my vision it appeared thus, that your petition will not be granted unto you [[throughout all the days of eternity, and that judgement has been finally passed upon you: yea (your petition) will not be granted unto you]]. 5. And from henceforth you shall not ascend into heaven unto all eternity, and [in bonds] of the earth the decree has gone forth to bind you for all the days of the world. 6. And (that) previously you shall have seen the destruction of your beloved sons and ye shall have no pleasure in them, but they shall fall before you by the sword. 7. And your petition on their behalf shall not be granted, nor yet on your own: even though you weep and pray and **speak all the words** contained in the writing which I have written. 8. And the vision was shown to me thus: Behold, in the vision clouds invited me and a mist summoned me, and the course of the stars and the lightnings sped and **hastened** me, and the winds in the vision caused me to fly and lifted me upward, and bore me into heaven. 9. And I went in till I drew nigh to a wall which is built of crystals and surrounded by tongues of fire: and it began to affright me. And I went into the tongues of fire and drew nigh to a large house which

was built of crystals: and the walls of the house were like a tesselated floor (made) of crystals, and its groundwork was of crystal.

11. Its ceiling was like the path of the stars and the lightnings, and between them were fiery cherubim, and their heaven was (clear as) water. 12. A flaming fire surrounded the walls, and its portals blazed with fire. 13. And I entered into that house, and it was hot as fire and cold as ice: there were no delights of life therein: fear covered me, and trembling got hold upon me. 14. And as I quaked and trembled, I fell upon my face. 15. And I beheld a vision, And lo! there was a second house, greater than the former, and the entire portal stood open before me, and it was built of flames of fire. 16. And in every respect it so excelled in splendour and magnificence and extent that I cannot describe to you its splendour and its extent. 17. And its floor was of fire, and above it were lightnings and the path of the stars, and its ceiling also was flaming fire. 18. And I looked and saw [[therein]] a lofty throne: its appearance was as crystal, and the wheels thereof as the shining sun, and there was the **vision** of cherubim. 19. And from underneath the throne came streams of flaming fire so that I could not look thereon. 20. And the Great Glory sat thereon, and His raiment shone more brightly than the sun and was whiter than any snow. 21. None of the angels could enter and could behold His face by reason of the magnificence and glory and no flesh could behold Him. 22. The flaming fire was round about Him, and a great fire stood before Him, and none around could draw nigh Him: ten thousand times ten thousand (stood) before Him, yet He needed no counselor. 23. And the most holy ones who were nigh to Him did not leave by night nor depart from Him. 24. And until then I had been prostrate on my face, trembling: and the Lord called me with His own mouth, and said to me: 'Come hither, Enoch, and hear my word.' 25. [And one of the holy ones came to me and waked me], and He made me rise up and approach the door: and I bowed my face downwards.

CHAPTER XV.

1. And He answered and said to me, and I heard His voice: 'Fear not, Enoch, thou righteous man and scribe of righteousness: approach hither and hear my voice. 2. And go, say to [[the Watchers of heaven]], who have sent thee to intercede [[for them: "You should intercede"]] for men, and not men for you: 3. Wherefore have ye left the high, holy, and eternal heaven, and lain with women, and defiled yourselves with the daughters of men and taken to yourselves wives, and done like the children of earth, and begotten giants (as your) sons? 4. And though ye were holy, spiritual, living the eternal life, you have defiled yourselves with the blood of women, and have begotten (children) with the blood of flesh, and, **as the children** of men, have lusted after flesh and blood as those [also] do who die and perish. 5. Therefore have I given them wives also that they might impregnate them, and beget children by them, that thus nothing might be wanting to them on earth. 6. But you were [formerly] spiritual, living the eternal life, and immortal for all generations of the world. 7. And therefore I have not appointed wives for you; for as for the spiritual ones of the heaven, in heaven is their dwelling. 8. And now, the giants, who are produced from the spirits and flesh, shall be called evil spirits upon the earth, and on the earth shall be their dwelling. 9. Evil spirits have proceeded from their bodies; because they are born from **men**, [[and]] from the holy Watchers is their beginning and primal origin;[they shall be evil spirits on earth, and] evil spirits shall they be called. [10. As for the spirits of heaven, in heaven shall be their dwelling, but as for the spirits of the earth which were born upon the earth, on the earth shall be their dwelling.] 11. And the spirits of the giants **afflict**, oppress, destroy, attack, do battle, and work destruction on the earth, and cause trouble: they take no food, [but nevertheless hunger] and thirst, and cause offences. And these spirits shall rise up against the

children of men and against the women, because they have proceeded [from them].

CHAPTER XVI.

1. From the days of the slaughter and destruction and death [of the giants], from the souls of whose flesh the spirits, having gone forth, shall destroy without incurring judgement--thus shall they destroy until the day of the consummation, the great [judgement] in which the age shall be consummated, over the Watchers and the godless, yea, shall be wholly consummated." 2. And now as to the Watchers who have sent thee to intercede for them, who had been [[aforetime]] in heaven, (say to them): "You have been in heaven, but [all] the mysteries had not yet been revealed to you, and you knew worthless ones, and these in the hardness of your hearts you have made known to the women, and through these mysteries women and men work much evil on earth." 4. Say to them therefore: "You have no peace."'

Enoch's Journeys through the Earth and Sheol

CHAPTER XVII.

1. And they took [and] brought me to a place in which those who were there were like flaming fire, and, when they wished, they appeared as men. 2. And they brought me to the place of darkness, and to a mountain the point of whose summit reached to heaven. 3. And I saw the places of the luminaries [and the treasuries of the stars] and of the thunder [and] in the **uttermost depths**, where were a fiery bow and arrows and their quiver, and [[a fiery sword]] and all the lightnings. 4. And they took me to the living waters, and to the fire of the west, which receives every setting of the sun. 5. And I came to a river of fire in which the fire flows like water and discharges itself into the great sea towards the west. 6. I saw the great rivers and came to the great[river and to the great] darkness, and went to the place where no flesh walks. 7. I saw the mountains of the darkness of winter and the place whence all the waters of the deep flow. 8. I saw the mouths of all the rivers of the earth and the mouth of the deep.

CHAPTER XVIII

1. I saw the treasuries of all the winds: I saw how He had furnished with them the whole creation and the firm foundations of the earth. 2. And I saw the corner-stone of the earth: I saw the four winds which bear [the earth and] the firmament of the heaven. 3. [[And I saw how the winds stretch out the vaults of heaven]], and have their station between heaven and earth: [[these are the pillars of the heaven]]. 4. I saw the winds of heaven which turn and bring the circumference of the sun and all the stars to their setting. 5. I saw the winds on the earth carrying the clouds: I saw[[the paths of the angels. I saw]] at the end of the earth the firmament of the heaven above. And I proceeded and saw a place which burns day and night, where there are seven mountains of magnificent stones, three towards the east, and three towards the south. 7. And as for those towards the east, ⟨one⟩ was of coloured stone, and one of pearl, and one of **jacinth**, and those towards the south of red stone. 8. But the middle one reached to heaven like the throne of God, of alabaster, and the summit of the throne was of sapphire. 9. And I saw a flaming fire. And beyond these mountains 10. is a region the end of the great earth: there the heavens were completed. 11. And I saw a deep abyss, with columns [[of heavenly fire, and among them I saw columns]] of fire fall, which were beyond measure alike towards the height and towards the depth. 12. And beyond that abyss I saw a place which had no firmament of the heaven above, and no firmly founded earth beneath it: there was no water upon it, and no birds, but it was a waste and horrible place. 13. I saw there seven stars like great burning mountains, and to me, when I inquired regarding them, 14. The angel said: 'This place is the end of heaven and earth: this has become a prison for the stars and the host of heaven. 15. And the stars which roll over the fire are they which have transgressed the commandment of the Lord in the beginning of their rising, because they did not come forth at their appointed times. 16. And

He was wroth with them, and bound them till the time when their guilt should be consummated (even) [for ten thousand years].'

CHAPTER XIX.

1. And Uriel said to me: 'Here shall stand the angels who have connected themselves with women, and their spirits assuming many different forms are defiling mankind and shall lead them astray into sacrificing to demons [[as gods]], (here shall they stand,) till [[the day of]] the great judgement in which they shall be judged till they are made an end of. 2. And the women also of the angels who went astray shall become sirens.' 3. And I, Enoch, alone saw the vision, the ends of all things: and no man shall see as I have seen.

CHAPTER XX.

1. And these are the names of the holy angels who watch. 2. Uriel, one of the holy angels, who is over the world and over Tartarus. 3. Raphael, one of the holy angels, who is over the spirits of men. 4. Raguel, one of the holy angels who †takes vengeance on† the world of the luminaries. 5. Michael, one of the holy angels, to wit, he that is set over the best part of mankind [[and]]over chaos. 6. Saraqâêl, one of the holy angels, who is set over the spirits, who sin in the spirit. 7. Gabriel, one of the holy angels, who is over Paradise and the serpents and the Cherubim. 8. Remiel, one of the holy angels, whom God set over those who rise.

CHAPTER XXI.

1. And I proceeded to where things were chaotic. 2. And I saw there something horrible: I saw neither a heaven above nor a firmly founded earth, but a place chaotic and horrible. 3. And there I saw seven stars of

the heaven bound together in it, like great mountains and burning with fire. 4. Then I said: 'For what sin are they bound, and on what account have they been cast in hither?' 5. Then said Uriel, one of the holy angels, who was with me, and was chief over them, and said: 'Enoch, why dost thou ask, and why art thou eager for the truth? 6. These are of the number of the stars [of heaven], which have transgressed the commandment of the Lord, and are bound here till ten thousand years, the time entailed by their sins, are consummated.' 7. And from thence I went to another place, which was still more horrible than the former, and I saw a horrible thing: a great fire there which burnt and blazed, and the place was cleft as far as the abyss, being full of great descending columns of fire: neither its extent or magnitude could I see, nor could I conjecture. 8. Then I said: 'How fearful is the place and how terrible to look upon!' 9. Then Uriel answered me, one of the holy angels who was with me, and said unto me: 'Enoch, why hast thou such fear and affright?' And I answered: 'Because of this fearful place, and because of the spectacle of the pain.' 10. And he said [[unto me]]: 'This place is the prison of the angels, and here they will be imprisoned for ever.'

CHAPTER XXII.

1. And thence I went to another place, and he showed me in the west [another] great and high mountain [and] of hard rock.

E

2 And there was in it †four† **hollow** places, deep and wide and very smooth. †How† smooth are **the hollow places** and deep and dark to look at.

Gg

2. And there were †four† hollow places in it, deep and very smooth: †three† of them were dark and one bright; and there was a fountain of

water in its midst. And I said: '†How† smooth are these hollow places, and deep and dark to view.'

3. Then Raphael answered, one of the holy angels who was with me, and said unto me: 'These hollow places have been created for this very purpose, that the spirits of the souls of the dead should assemble therein, yea that all the souls of the children of men should assemble here. And these places **have been made** to receive them till the day of their judgement and till their appointed period [till the period appointed], till the great judgement (comes) upon them.'

E

5. I saw the spirits of the children of men who were dead, and their voice went forth to heaven and made suit.

6. Then I asked Raphael the angel who was with me, and I said unto him: 'This spirit--whose is it whose voice goeth forth and maketh suit?'

Gg

5. I saw (the spirit of) **a dead man** making suit, and his voice went forth to heaven and made suit.

6. And I asked Raphael the angel who was with me, and I said unto him: 'This spirit which maketh suit, whose is it, whose voice goeth forth and maketh suit to heaven?'

7. And he answered me saying: 'This is the spirit which went forth from Abel, whom his brother Cain slew, and he makes his suit against him till his seed is destroyed from the face of the earth, and his seed is annihilated from amongst the seed of men.'

8. Then I asked regarding it, and regarding all the **hollow places**: 'Why as one separated from the other?'

Gg

8. Then I asked regarding all the **hollow places**: 'Why is one separated from the other?'

E

9. And he answered me and said unto me: 'These three have been made that the spirits of the dead might be separated. And such a division has been made ⟨for⟩ the spirits of the righteous, in which there as the **bright** spring of **water**.

10. **And** such has been made for sinners when they die and are buried in the earth and judgement has not been executed on them in their lifetime.

11. Here their spirits shall be set apart in this great pain till the great day of judgement and punishment and torment of those who †curse† for ever, and retribution for their spirits. There He shall bind them for ever.

12. And such a division has been made for the spirits of those who make their suit, who make disclosures concerning their destruction, when they were slain in the days of the sinners.

13. Such has been made for the spirits of men who were not righteous but sinners, who were complete in transgression, and of the transgressors. they shall be companions: but their spirits shall not be slain in the day of judgement nor shall they be raised from thence.

14. Then I blessed the Lord of glory and said: 'Blessed be my Lord, the Lord of righteousness, who ruleth for ever.'

Gg

9. And he answered me saying: 'These three have been made that the spirits of the dead might be separated. And **this** division has been made for the spirits of the righteous, in which there is the bright spring of water.

10. And **this** has been made for sinners when they die and are buried in the earth and judgement has not been executed upon them in their lifetime.

11. Here their spirits shall be set apart in this great pain, till the great day of judgement, scourgings, and torments of the accursed for ever, **so that** (there maybe) retribution for their spirits. There He shall bind them for ever.

12. And **this** division has been made for the spirits of those who make their suit, who make disclosures concerning their destruction, when they were slain in the days of the sinners.

13. And **this** has been made for the spirits of men who shall not be righteous but sinners, who are godless, and of the lawless they shall be companions: but their spirits shall not be punished in the day of judgement nor shall they be raised from thence.

14. Then I blessed the Lord of Glory and said: 'Blessed art Thou, Lord of righteousness, who rulest over the world.'

CHAPTER XXIII.

1. From thence I went to another place to the west of the ends of the earth. 2. And I saw a [[burning]] fire which ran without resting, and paused not from its course day or night but (ran) regularly. 3. And I asked saying: 'What is this which rests not?' 4. Then Raguel, one of the holy angels who was with me, answered me [[and said unto me]]: 'This course [of fire] [[which thou hast seen]] is the fire in the west which †persecutes† all the luminaries of heaven.'

CHAPTER XXIV.

1. [[And from thence I went to another place of the earth]], and he showed me a mountain range of fire which burnt [[day and night]]. 2. And I went beyond it and saw seven magnificent mountains all differing each from the other, and the stones (thereof) were magnificent and beautiful, magnificent as a whole, of glorious appearance and fair exterior: [[three towards]] the east,[[one]] founded on the other, and three towards the south, one upon the other, and deep rough ravines, no

one of which joined with any other. 3. And the seventh mountain was in the midst of these, and it excelled them in height, resembling the seat of a throne: and fragrant trees encircled the throne. 4. And amongst them was a tree such as I had never yet smelt, neither was any amongst them nor were others like it: it had a fragrance beyond all fragrance, and its leaves and blooms and wood wither not for ever: and its fruit [[is beautiful, and its fruit]] resembles the dates of a palm. 5. Then I said:

'[How] beautiful is this tree, and fragrant, and its leaves are fair, and its

blooms [[very]] delightful in appearance.' 6. Then answered Michael, one of the holy[[and honoured]] angels who was with me, and was their leader.

CHAPTER XXV.

1. And he said unto me: 'Enoch, why dost thou ask me regarding the fragrance of the tree, and [why] dost thou wish to learn the truth?' Then I answered him [[saying]]: 'I wish to know about everything, but especially about this tree.' And he answered saying: 'This high mountain [[which thou hast seen]], whose summit is like the throne of God, is His throne, where the Holy Great One, the Lord of Glory, the Eternal King, will sit, when He shall come down to visit the earth with goodness. 4. And as for this fragrant tree no mortal is permitted to touch it till the great judgement, when He shall take vengeance on all and bring

(everything) to its consummation for ever. It shall then be given to the righteous and holy. 5. Its fruit **shall be** for food to the elect: it shall be transplanted to the holy place, to the temple of the Lord, the Eternal King.

6 Then shall they rejoice with joy and be glad,
And into the holy place shall they enter;

And its fragrance shall be in their bones, And they shall live a long life on earth, Such as thy fathers lived:

And in their days shall no [[sorrow or]] plague Or torment or calamity touch them.'

7 Then blessed I the God of Glory, the Eternal King, who hath prepared such things for the righteous, and hath created them and promised to give to them.

CHAPTER XXVI.

1. And I went from thence to the middle of the earth, and I saw a blessed place [in which there were trees] with branches abiding and blooming [of a dismembered tree]. 2. And there I saw a holy mountain, [[and]] underneath the mountain to the east there was a stream and it flowed towards the south. 3. And I saw towards the east another mountain higher than this, and between them a deep and narrow ravine: in it also ran a stream [underneath] the mountain. 4. And to the west thereof there was another mountain, lower than the former and of small elevation, and a ravine [deep and dry] between them: and another deep and dry ravine was at the extremities of the three [mountains]. 5. And all the ravines were deep [[and narrow]], (being formed) of hard rock, and trees were not planted upon them. 6. And I marveled [[at the rocks, and I marveled]] at the ravine, yea, I marveled very much.

CHAPTER XXVII.

1. Then said I: 'For what object is this blessed land, which is entirely filled with trees, and this accursed valley [[between]]?' 2. [[Then Uriel, one of the holy angels who was with me, answered and said: 'This]] accursed valley is for those who are accursed for ever: Here shall all [the accursed]

be gathered together who utter with their lips against the Lord unseemly words and of His glory speak hard things.

E

Here shall they be gathered together, and here shall be their place of judgement. 3. In the last days there shall be upon them the spectacle of righteous judgement in the presence of the righteous for ever: here shall the merciful bless the Lord of glory, the Eternal King.

Gg

Here shall they be gathered together, and here shall be the place of their habitation. 3. In the last times, in the days of the true judgement in the presence of the righteous for ever: here shall the **godly** bless the Lord of Glory, the Eternal Kin.

4. In the days of judgement over the former, they shall bless Him for the mercy in accordance with which He has assigned them (their lot).' 5. Then I blessed the Lord of Glory and set forth His [glory] and lauded Him gloriously.

CHAPTER XXVIII

1. And thence I went [[towards the east]], into the midst [[of the mountain range of the desert]], and I saw a wilderness and it was solitary, full of trees **and plants**. 2. [[And]] water gushed forth from above. 3. Rushing like a copious watercourse [which flowed] towards the north-west it caused clouds and dew to ascend on every side.

CHAPTER XXIX.

1. And thence I went to another place in the desert, and approached to the east of this mountain range. 2. And [[there]] I saw **aromatic** trees

exhaling the fragrance of frankincense and myrrh, and the trees also were similar to the almond tree.

CHAPTER XXX.

1 .And beyond these, I went afar to the east, and I saw another place, a valley (full) of water.

2. And [therein there was] a tree, the colour (?) of fragrant trees such as the mastic. 3. And on the sides of those valleys I saw fragrant cinnamon. And beyond these I proceeded to the east.

CHAPTER XXXI.

1. And I saw other mountains, and amongst them were [groves of] trees, and there flowed forth from them nectar, which is named sarara and galbanum. 2. And beyond these mountains I saw another mountain [to the east of the ends of the earth], [[whereon were aloe trees]], and all the trees were full **of stacte**, being like almond-trees. 3. And when one **burnt** it, it smelt sweeter than any fragrant odour.

CHAPTER XXXII.

E

1. And after these fragrant odours, as I looked towards the north over the mountains I saw seven mountains full of choice nard and fragrant trees and cinnamon and pepper.

Gg

1. To the north-east I beheld seven mountains full of choice nard and mastic and cinnamon and pepper.

2. And thence I went over the summits of [all] these mountains, far towards the east [of the earth], and passed above the Erythraean sea and went far from it, and passed over [[the angel]] Zotîêl.

E

3. And I came to the Garden of Righteousness, and saw beyond those trees many large trees growing there and of goodly fragrance, large, very beautiful and glorious, and the tree of wisdom whereof they eat and know great wisdom.

Gg

3. And I came to the Garden of Righteousness, and from afar off trees more numerous than these trees and great--†two† trees there, very great, beautiful, and glorious, and magnificent, and the tree of knowledge, whose holy fruit they eat and know great wisdom.

4. [That tree is in height like the fir, and its leaves are] like (those of) the Carob tree: and its fruit is like the clusters of the vine, very beautiful: and the fragrance of the tree penetrates afar. 5. Then I said: '[How] beautiful is the tree, and how attractive is its look!' 6. Then Raphael the holy angel, who was with me, answered me [[and said]]: 'This is the tree of wisdom, of which thy father old (in years) and thy aged mother, who were before thee, have eaten, and they learnt wisdom and their eyes were opened, and they knew that they were naked and they were driven out of the garden.'

CHAPTER XXXIII.

1. And from thence I went to the ends of the earth and saw there great beasts, and each differed from the other; and (I saw) birds also differing in appearance and beauty and voice, the one differing from the other. 2. And to the east of those beasts I saw the ends of the earth whereon the heaven rests, and the portals of the heaven open. 3. And I saw how the stars of heaven come forth, and I counted the portals out of which they proceed, and wrote down all their outlets, of each individual star by itself, according to their number and their names, their courses and their

positions, and their times and their months, as Uriel the holy angel who was with me showed me. 4. He showed all things to me and wrote them down for me: also their names he wrote for me, and their laws and their companies.

CHAPTER XXXIV.

1. And from thence I went towards the north to the ends of the earth, and there I saw a great and glorious device at the ends of the whole earth. 2. And here I saw three portals of heaven open in the heaven: through each of them proceed north winds: when they blow there is cold, hail, frost, snow, dew, and rain. 3. And out of one portal they blow for good: but when they blow through the other two portals, it is with violence and affliction on the earth, and they blow with violence.

CHAPTER XXXV.

1. And from thence I went towards the west to the ends of the earth, and saw there three portals of the heaven open such as I had seen in the †east†, the same number of portals, and the same number of outlets.

CHAPTER XXXVI.

1. And from thence I went to the south to the ends of the earth, and saw there three open portals of the heaven: and thence there come dew, rain, †and wind†. 2. And from thence I went to the east to the ends of the heaven, and saw here the three eastern portals of heaven open and small portals above them. 3. Through each of these small portals pass the stars of heaven and run their course to the west on the path which is shown to them. 4. And as often as I saw I blessed always the Lord of Glory, and I continued to bless the Lord of Glory who has wrought great and glorious wonders, to show the greatness of His work to the angels and to **spirits** and to men, that they might praise His work and all His creation: that

they might see the work of His might and praise the great work of His hands and bless Him for ever.

THE PARABLES

SECTION II. CHAPTERS 37-71

CHAPTER XXXVII.

1. The second vision which he saw, the vision of wisdom--which Enoch the son of Jared, the son of Mahalalel, the son of Cainan, the son of Enos, the son of Seth, the son of Adam, saw.

2. And this is the beginning of the words of wisdom which I lifted up my voice to speak and say to those which dwell on earth: Hear, ye men of old time, and see, ye that come after, the words of the Holy One which I will speak before the Lord of Spirits. 3. It were better to declare (them only) to the men of old time, but even from those that come after we will not withhold the beginning of wisdom. 4. Till the present day such wisdom has never been given **by** the Lord of Spirits as I have received according to my insight, according to the good pleasure of the Lord of Spirits by whom the lot of eternal life has been given to me. 5. Now three parables were imparted to me, and I lifted up my voice and recounted them to those that dwell on the earth.

THE FIRST PARABLE

CHAPTER XXXVIII

1. The First Parable.

When the congregation of the righteous shall appear, And sinners shall be judged for their sins, And shall be driven from the face of the earth:

2. And when the Righteous One shall appear before the eyes of the righteous,

Whose elect works hang upon the Lord of Spirits,

And light shall appear to the righteous and the elect who dwell on the earth,

Where then will be the dwelling of the sinners,

And where the resting-place of those who have denied the Lord of Spirits? It had been good for them if they had not been born.

3. When the secrets of the righteous shall be revealed and the sinners judged,

And the godless driven from the presence of the righteous and elect,

4. From that time those that possess the earth shall no longer be powerful and exalted:

And they shall not be able to behold the face of the holy, For the Lord of Spirits has **caused His light to**

appear On the face of the holy,
righteous, and elect.

5. Then shall the kings and the mighty perish

And be given into the hands of the righteous and holy.

6. And thenceforward none shall seek for themselves mercy from the Lord of Spirits For their life is at an end.

CHAPTER XXXIX.

1. [And it †shall come to pass in those days that elect and holy children †will descend from the high heaven, and their seed †will become one with the children of men. 2. And in those days Enoch received books of zeal and wrath, and books of disquiet and expulsion.]

And mercy shall not be accorded to them, saith the Lord of Spirits. 3. And in those days a whirlwind carried me off from the earth, And set me down at the end of the heavens.

4. And there I saw another vision, the dwelling-places of the holy, And the resting-places of the righteous.

5. Here mine eyes saw their dwellings with His righteous angels, And their resting-places with the holy.

And they petitioned and interceded and prayed for the children of men, And righteousness flowed before them as water,

And mercy like dew upon the earth:

Thus it is amongst them for ever and ever.

6*a*. And in that place mine eyes saw the Elect One of righteousness and of faith, 7*a*. And I saw his dwelling-place under the wings of the Lord of Spirits.

6*b*. And righteousness shall prevail in his days,

And the righteous and elect shall be without number before Him for ever and ever.

7*b*. And all the righteous and elect before Him shall be †strong† as fiery lights, And their mouth shall be full of blessing,

And their lips extol the name of the Lord of Spirits,

And righteousness before Him shall never fail,

[And uprightness shall never fail before Him.]

8. There I wished to dwell,
And my spirit longed for that dwelling-place:

And there heretofore hath been my portion,

For so has it been established concerning me before the Lord of Spirits.

9. In those days I praised and extolled the name of the Lord of Spirits with blessings and praises, because He hath destined me for blessing and glory according to the good pleasure of the Lord of Spirits. 10. For a long time my eyes regarded that place, and I blessed Him and praised Him, saying: 'Blessed is He, and may He be blessed from the beginning and for evermore. 11. And before Him there is no ceasing. He knows before the world was created what is for ever and what will be from generation unto generation. 12. Those who sleep not bless Thee: they stand before Thy glory and bless, praise, and extol, saying: "Holy, holy, holy, is the Lord of Spirits: He filleth the earth with spirits."' 13. And here my eyes saw all those who sleep not: they stand before Him and bless and say: 'Blessed be Thou, and blessed be the name of the Lord

for ever and ever.' 14. And my face was changed; for I could no longer behold.

CHAPTER XL.

1. And after that I saw thousands of thousands and ten thousand times ten thousand, I saw a multitude beyond number and reckoning, who stood before the Lord of Spirits. 2. And on the four sides of the Lord of Spirits I saw four presences, different from those that sleep not, and I learnt their names: for the angel that went with me made known to me their names, and showed me all the hidden things.

3. And I heard the voices of those four presences as they uttered praises before the Lord of glory. 4. The first voice blesses the Lord of Spirits for ever and ever. 5. And the second voice I heard blessing the Elect One and the elect ones who hang upon the Lord of Spirits. 6. And the third voice I heard **pray and intercede** for those who dwell on the earth and **supplicate** in the name of the Lord of Spirits. 7. And I heard the fourth voice fending off the Satans and forbidding them to come before the Lord of Spirits to accuse them who dwell on the earth. 8. After that I asked the angel of peace who went with me, who showed me everything that is hidden: 'Who are these four presences which I have seen and whose words I have heard and written down?' 9. And he said to me: 'This first is Michael, the merciful and long-suffering: and the second, who is set over all the diseases and all the wounds of the children of men, is Raphael: and the third, who is set over all the powers, is Gabriel: and the fourth, who is set over the repentance unto hope of those who inherit eternal life, is named Phanuel.' And these are the four angels of the Lord of Spirits and the four voices I heard in those days.

CHAPTER XLI.

1. And after that I saw all the secrets of the heavens, and how the kingdom is divided, and how the actions of men are weighed in the balance. 2. And there I saw the mansions of the elect and the mansions of the holy, and mine eyes saw there all the sinners being driven from thence which deny the name of the Lord of Spirits, and being dragged off: and they could not abide because of the punishment which proceeds from the Lord of Spirits.

3. And there mine eyes saw the secrets of the lightning and of the thunder, and the secrets of the winds, how they are divided to blow over the earth, and the secrets of the clouds and dew, and there I saw from whence they proceed in that place and from whence they saturate the dusty earth. 4. And there I saw closed chambers out of which the winds are divided, the chamber of the hail and winds, the chamber of the mist, and of the clouds, and the cloud thereof hovers over the earth from the beginning of the world. 5. And I saw the chambers of the sun and moon, whence they proceed and whither they come again, and their glorious return, and how one is superior to the other, and their stately orbit, and how they do not leave their orbit, and they add nothing to their orbit and they take nothing from it, and they keep faith with each other, in accordance with the oath by which they are bound together. 6. And first the sun goes forth and traverses his path according to the commandment of the Lord of Spirits, and mighty is His name for ever and ever. 7. And after that I saw the hidden and the visible path of the moon, and she accomplishes the course of her path in that place by day and by night--the one holding a position opposite to the other before the Lord of Spirits.

And they give thanks and praise and rest not; For unto them is their thanksgiving rest.

8. For the sun changes oft for a blessing or a curse,

And the course of the path of the moon is light to the righteous And darkness to the sinners in the name of the Lord,

Who made a separation between the light and the darkness, And divided the spirits of men,

And strengthened the spirits of the righteous, In the name of His righteousness.

9. For no angel hinders and no power is able to hinder; for He appoints a judge for them all and He judges them all before Him.

CHAPTER XLII.

1. Wisdom found no place where she might dwell; Then a dwelling-place was assigned her in the heavens.

2 Wisdom went forth to make her dwelling among the children of men, And found no dwelling-place:

Wisdom returned to her place,

And took her seat among the angels.

3 And unrighteousness went forth from her chambers:

Whom she sought not she found, And dwelt with them,

As rain in a desert

And dew on a thirsty land.

CHAPTER XLIII.

1. And I saw other lightnings and the stars of heaven, and I saw how He called them all by their names and they hearkened unto Him. 2. And I saw how they are weighed in a righteous balance according to their proportions of light: (I saw) the width of their spaces and the day of their appearing, and how their revolution produces lightning: and (I saw) their revolution according to the number of the angels, and (how) they keep faith with each other. 3. And I asked the angel who went with me who showed me what was hidden: 'What are these?' 4. And he said to me: 'The Lord of Spirits hath showed thee their parabolic meaning (lit. 'their parable'): these are the names of the holy who dwell on the earth and believe in the name of the Lord of Spirits for ever and ever.'

CHAPTER XLIV.

Also another phenomenon I saw in regard to the lightnings: how some of the stars arise and become lightnings and cannot part with their new form.

THE SECOND PARABLE

CHAPTER XLV.

1. And this is the Second Parable concerning those who
deny the name of the dwelling of the holy ones and the
Lord of Spirits.

2. And into the heaven they shall not ascend, And on the earth they shall not come:

Such shall be the lot of the sinners

Who have denied the name of the Lord of Spirits,

Who are thus preserved for the day of suffering and tribulation.

3. On that day Mine Elect One shall sit on the throne of glory And shall **try** their works,

And their places of rest shall be innumerable.

And their souls shall grow strong within them when they see Mine Elect Ones, And those who have called upon My glorious name:

4. Then will I cause Mine Elect One to dwell among them.

And I will transform the heaven and make it an eternal blessing and light 5. And I will transform the earth and make it a blessing:

And I will cause Mine elect ones to dwell upon it:

But the sinners and evil-doers shall not set foot thereon.

6. For I have provided and satisfied with peace My righteous ones And have caused them to dwell before Me:

But for the sinners there is judgement impending with Me, So that I shall destroy them from the face of the earth.

CHAPTER XLVI.

1. And there I saw One who had a head of days,

And His head was white like wool,

And with Him was another being whose countenance had the appearance of a man, And his face was full of graciousness, like one of the holy angels.

2. And I asked the **angel** who went with me and showed me all the hidden things, concerning that Son of Man, who he was, and whence he was, (and) why he went with the Head of Days? And he answered and said unto me:

This is the son of Man who hath righteousness,

With whom dwelleth righteousness,

And who revealeth all the treasures of that which is hidden,

Because the Lord of Spirits hath chosen him,

And whose lot hath the pre-eminence before the Lord of Spirits in uprightness for ever.

4, And this Son of Man whom thou hast seen

Shall †raise up† the kings and the mighty from their seats,

[And the strong from their thrones]

And shall loosen the reins of the strong,
And break the teeth of the sinners.

5. [And he shall put down the kings from their thrones and kingdoms]

Because they do not extol and praise Him,

Nor humbly acknowledge whence the kingdom was bestowed upon them. 6. And he shall put down the countenance of the strong, And shall fill them with shame.

And darkness shall be their dwelling,

And worms shall be their bed,

And they shall have no hope of rising from their beds, Because they do not extol the name of the Lord of Spirits.

7. And these are they who †judge† the stars of heaven, [And raise their hands against the Most High], †And tread upon the earth and dwell upon it†.

And all their deeds manifest unrighteousness, And their power rests upon their riches,

And their faith is in the †gods† which they have made with their hands, And they deny the name of the Lord of Spirits,

8. And they persecute the houses of His congregations, And the faithful who hang upon the name of the Lord of Spirits.

CHAPTER XLVII.

1. And in those days shall have ascended the prayer of the righteous, And the blood of the righteous from the earth before the Lord of Spirits.

2. In those days the holy ones who dwell above in the heavens

Shall unite with one voice

And supplicate and pray [and praise,

And give thanks and bless the name of the Lord of Spirits]

On behalf of the blood of the righteous which has been shed,

And that the prayer of the righteous may not be in vain before the Lord of Spirits, That judgement may be done unto them, And that they may not have to suffer for ever.

3. In those days I saw the Head of Days when He seated himself upon the throne of His glory, And the books of the living were opened before Him:

And all His host which is in heaven above and His counselors stood before Him,

4 And the hearts of the holy were filled with joy;

Because the number of the righteous **had been offered**,

And the prayer of the righteous had been heard,

And the blood of the righteous been required before the Lord of Spirits.

CHAPTER XLVIII.

1. And in that place I saw the fountain of righteousness
Which was inexhaustible:

And around it were many fountains of wisdom;

And all the thirsty drank of them,

And were filled with wisdom,

And their dwellings were with the righteous and holy and elect.

2. And at that hour that Son of Man was named In the presence of the Lord of Spirits, And his name before the Head of Days.

3. Yea, before the sun and the signs were created, Before the stars of the heaven were made, His name was named before the Lord of Spirits.

4. He shall be a staff to the righteous whereon to stay themselves and not fall,

And he shall be the light of the Gentiles,

And the hope of those who are troubled of heart.

5. All who dwell on earth shall fall down and worship before him, And will praise and bless and celebrate with song the Lord of Spirits.

6. And for this reason hath he been chosen and hidden before Him, Before the creation of the world and for evermore.

7. And the wisdom of the Lord of Spirits hath revealed him to the holy and righteous;

For he hath preserved the lot of the righteous,

Because they have hated and despised this world of unrighteousness, And have hated all its works and ways in the name of the Lord of Spirits:

For in his name they are saved,

And according to his good pleasure hath it been in regard to their life.

8. In these days downcast in countenance shall the kings of the earth have become, And the strong who possess the land because of the works of their hands;

For on the day of their anguish and affliction they shall not (be able to) save themselves.

9. And I will give them over into the hands of Mine elect:

As straw in the fire so shall they burn before
the face of the holy: As lead in the water shall
they sink before the face of the righteous, And
no trace of them shall any more be found.

10. And on the day of their affliction there shall be rest on the earth, And before them they shall fall and not rise again:

And there shall be no one to take them with his hands and raise them:

For they have denied the Lord of Spirits and His Anointed.

The name of the Lord of Spirits be blessed.

CHAPTER XLIX.

l. For wisdom is poured out like water,

And glory faileth not before him for evermore.

2. For he is mighty in all the secrets of righteousness,

And unrighteousness shall disappear as a shadow,

And have no continuance;

Because the Elect One standeth
before the Lord of Spirits, And his

glory is for ever and ever, And his
might unto all generations.

3. And in him dwells the spirit of wisdom,

And the spirit which gives insight,

And the spirit of understanding and of might,

And the spirit of those who have fallen asleep in righteousness.

4. And he shall judge the secret things,

And none shall be able to utter a lying word before him;

For he is the Elect One before the Lord of Spirits according to His good pleasure.

CHAPTER L.

1. And in those days a change shall take place for the holy and elect,

And the light of days shall abide upon them,

And glory and honour shall turn to the holy,

2. On the day of affliction on which evil shall have been treasured up against the sinners.

And the righteous shall be victorious in the name of the Lord of Spirits:

And He will cause the others to witness (this)

That they may repent

And forgo the works of their hands.

3. They shall have no honour through the name of the Lord of Spirits,

Yet through His name shall they be saved,

And the Lord of Spirits will have compassion on them, For His compassion is great.

4. And He is righteous also in His judgement,

And in the presence of His glory unrighteousness also shall not maintain itself:

At His judgement the unrepentant shall perish before Him.

5. And from henceforth I will have no mercy on them, saith the Lord of Spirits.

CHAPTER LI.

1. And in those days shall the earth also give back that which has been entrusted to it, And Sheol also shall give back that which it has received, And hell shall give back that which it owes.

5*a*. For in those days the Elect One shall arise,

2. And he shall choose the righteous and holy from among them: For the day has drawn nigh that they should be saved.

3. And the Elect One shall in those days sit on My throne,

And his mouth shall **pour** forth all the secrets of wisdom and counsel:

For the Lord of Spirits hath given (them) to him and hath glorified him.

4. And in those days shall the mountains leap like rams,

And the hills also shall skip like lambs satisfied with milk,

And the faces of [all] the angels in heaven shall be lighted up with joy.

5*b*. And the earth shall rejoice,

c. And the righteous shall dwell upon it,

d. And the elect shall walk thereon.

CHAPTER LII.

l. And after those days in that place where I had seen all the visions of that which is hidden-for I had been carried off in a whirlwind and they had borne me towards the west-- 2. There mine eyes saw all the secret things of heaven that shall be, a mountain of iron, and a mountain of copper, and a mountain of silver, and a mountain of gold, and a mountain of soft metal, and a mountain of lead.

3. And I asked the angel who went with me, saying, 'What things are these which I have seen in secret?' 4. And he said unto me: 'All these things which thou hast seen shall serve the dominion of His Anointed that he may be potent and mighty on the earth.'

5. And that angel of peace answered, saying unto me: 'Wait a little, and there shall be revealed unto thee all the secret things which surround the Lord of Spirits.

6. And these mountains which thine eyes have seen,

The mountain of iron, and the mountain of copper, and the mountain of silver,

And the mountain of gold, and the mountain of soft metal, and the mountain of lead,

All these shall be in the presence of the Elect One

As wax: before the fire,

And like the water which streams down from above [upon those mountains], And they shall become powerless before his feet.

7. And it shall come to pass in those days that none shall be saved, Either by gold or by silver, And none be able to escape.

8 And there shall be no iron for war,

Nor shall one clothe oneself with a breastplate.

Bronze shall be of no service,

And tin [shall be of no service and] shall
not be esteemed, And lead shall not be
desired.

9 And all these things shall be [denied and] destroyed from the surface of the earth, When the Elect One shall appear before the face of the Lord of Spirits.'

CHAPTER LIII.

1. There mine eyes saw a deep valley with open mouths, and all who dwell on the earth and sea and islands shall bring to him gifts and presents and tokens of homage, but that deep valley shall not become full.

2. And their hands commit lawless deeds,

And the sinners devour all whom they lawlessly **oppress**:

Yet the sinners shall be destroyed before the face
of the Lord of Spirits, And they shall be banished
from off the face of His earth, And they shall
perish for ever and ever.

3. For I saw all the angels of punishment abiding (there) and preparing all the instruments of Satan. 4. And I asked the angel of peace who went with me: 'For whom are they preparing these instruments?' 5. And he said unto me: 'They prepare these for the kings and the mighty of this earth, that they may thereby be destroyed.

6. And after this the Righteous and Elect One shall cause the house of his congregation to appear: henceforth they shall be no more hindered in the name of the Lord of Spirits.

7. And these mountains shall not stand as the earth before his righteousness,

But the hills shall be as a fountain of water,

And the righteous shall have rest from the oppression of sinners.'

CHAPTER LIV.

1 And I looked and turned to another part of the earth, and saw there a deep valley with burning fire. 2. And they brought the kings and the mighty, and began to cast them into this deep valley. 3. And there mine eyes saw how they made these their instruments, iron chains of immeasurable weight. 4. And I asked the angel of peace who went with me, saying: 'For whom are these chains being prepared?' 5. And he said unto me: 'These are being prepared for the hosts of Azâzêl, so that they may take them and cast them into the abyss of complete condemnation, and they shall cover their jaws with rough stones as the Lord of Spirits commanded.

6. And Michael, and Gabriel, and Raphael, and Phanuel shall take hold of them on that great day, and cast them on that day into the burning furnace, that the Lord of Spirits may take vengeance on them for their unrighteousness in becoming subject to Satan and leading astray those who dwell on the earth.'

7. 'And in those days shall punishment come from the Lord of Spirits, and he will open all the chambers of waters which are above the heavens, and of the fountains which are beneath the earth. 8. And all the waters shall be joined with the waters: that which is above the heavens is the masculine, and the water which is beneath the earth is the feminine. 9. And they shall destroy all who dwell on the earth and those who dwell under the ends of the heaven. 10. And **when** they have recognized their

unrighteousness which they have wrought on the earth, then by these shall they perish.

CHAPTER LV.

1. And after that the Head of Days repented and said: 'In vain have I destroyed all who dwell on the earth.' 2. And He sware by His great name: 'Henceforth I will not do so to all who dwell on the earth, and I will set a sign in the heaven: and this shall be a pledge of good faith between Me and them for ever, so long as heaven is above the earth. And this is in accordance with My command.'

3. When I have desired to take hold of them by the hand of the angels on the day of tribulation and pain **because of** this, I will cause My chastisement and My wrath to abide upon them, saith God, the Lord of Spirits. 4. Ye †mighty kings† who dwell on the earth, ye shall have to behold Mine Elect One, how he sits on the throne of glory and judges Azâzêl, and all his associates, and all his hosts in the name of the Lord of Spirits.'

CHAPTER LVI.

1. And I saw there the hosts of the angels of punishment going, and they held scourges and chains of iron and bronze. 2. And I asked the angel of peace who went with me, saying: 'To whom are these who hold the scourges going?' 3. And he said unto me: 'To their elect and beloved ones, that they may be cast into the chasm of the abyss of the valley.

4. And then that valley shall be filled with their elect and beloved,

And the days of their lives shall be at an end,

And the days of their leading astray shall not thenceforward be reckoned.

5. And in those days the angels shall return

And hurl themselves to the east upon the Parthians and Medes:

They shall stir up the kings, so that a spirit of unrest shall come upon them,

And they shall rouse them from their thrones, That they may break forth as lions from their lairs, And as hungry wolves among their flocks.

6. And they shall go up and tread under foot the land of His elect ones,

[And the land of His elect ones shall be before them a threshing-
floor and a highway:] 7 But the city of my righteous shall be a
hindrance to their horses.

And they shall begin to fight among themselves,

And their right hand shall be strong against themselves,

And a man shall not know his brother, Nor a son his father or his mother,

Till there be no number of the corpses through their slaughter, And their punishment be not in vain.

8 In those days Sheol shall open its jaws, And they shall be swallowed up therein

And their destruction shall be at an end;

Sheol shall devour the sinners in the presence of the elect.'

CHAPTER LVII.

1. And it came to pass after this that I saw another host of wagons, and men riding thereon, and coming on the winds from the east, and from the west to the south. 2. And the noise of their wagons was heard, and

when this turmoil took place the holy ones from heaven remarked it, and the pillars of the earth were moved from their place, and the sound thereof was heard from the one end of heaven to the other, in one day. 3. And they shall all fall down and worship the Lord of Spirits. And this is the end of the second Parable.

The Third Parable

CHAPTER LVIII.

1. And I began to speak the third Parable concerning the righteous and elect.

2. Blessed are ye, ye righteous and elect, For glorious shall be your lot.

3. And the righteous shall be in the light of the sun. And the elect in the light of eternal life:

The days of their life shall be unending,

And the days of the holy without number.

4. And they shall seek the light and find righteousness with the Lord of Spirits: There shall be peace to the righteous in the name of the Eternal Lord.

5. And after this it shall be said to the holy in heaven

That they should seek out the secrets of righteousness, the heritage of faith: For it has become bright as the sun upon earth, And the darkness is past.

6. And there shall be a light that never **endeth**,

And to a limit (lit. 'number') of days they shall not come,

For the darkness shall first have been destroyed,

[And the light established before the Lord of Spirits]

And the light of uprightness established for ever before the Lord of Spirits.

CHAPTER LIX.

[1. In those days mine eyes saw the secrets of the lightnings, and of the lights, and the judgements they execute (lit. 'their judgement'): and they lighten for a blessing or a curse as the Lord of Spirits willeth. 2. And there I saw the secrets of the thunder, and how when it resounds above in the heaven, the sound thereof is heard, and he caused me to see the judgements executed on the earth, whether they be for well-being and blessing, or for a curse according to the word of the Lord of Spirits. 3. And after that all the secrets of the lights and lightnings were shown to me, and they lighten for blessing and for satisfying.]

Book Of Noah - A Fragment

CHAPTER LX.

1. In the year five hundred, in the seventh month, on the fourteenth day of the month in the life of †Enoch†. In that Parable I saw how a mighty quaking made the heaven of heavens to quake, and the host of the Most High, and the angels, a thousand thousands and ten thousand times **ten** thousand, were disquieted with a great disquiet. 2. And the Head of Days sat on the throne of His glory, and the angels and the righteous stood around Him.

3. And a great trembling seized me,

And fear took hold of me,

And my loins gave way,

And dissolved were my reins, And I fell upon my face.

4 And Michael sent another angel from among the holy ones and he raised me up, and when he had raised me up my spirit returned; for I had not been able to endure the look of this host, and the commotion and the quaking of the heaven. And Michael said unto me: 'Why art thou disquieted with such a vision? Until this day lasted the day of His mercy; and He hath been merciful and long-suffering towards those who dwell on the earth. 6. And when the day, and the power, and the punishment, and the judgement come, which the Lord of Spirits hath prepared for those who worship not the righteous **law**, and for those who deny the righteous judgement, and for those who take His name in vain--that day is prepared, for the elect a covenant, but for sinners an inquisition.

25. When the punishment of the Lord of Spirits shall rest upon them, it shall rest in order that the punishment of the Lord of Spirits may not come, in vain, and it shall slay the children with their mothers and the children with their fathers. Afterwards the judgement shall take place according to His mercy and His patience.'

7. And on that day were two monsters parted, a female monster named Leviathan, to dwell in the abysses of the ocean over the fountains of the waters. 8. But the male is named Behemoth, who occupied with his breast a waste wilderness named †Dûidâin†, on the east of the garden where the elect and righteous dwell, where my grandfather was taken up, the seventh from Adam, the first man whom the Lord of Spirits created. 9. And I besought the other angel that he should show me the might of those monsters, how they were parted on one day and cast, the one into the abysses of the sea, and the other unto the dry land of the wilderness. 10. And he said to me: 'Thou son of man, herein thou dost seek to know what is hidden.'

11. And the other angel who went with me and showed me what was hidden told me what is first and last in the heaven in the height, and beneath the earth in the depth, and at the ends of the heaven, and on the foundation of the heaven. 12. And the chambers of the winds, and how the winds are divided, and how they are weighed, and (how) the **portals** of the winds are reckoned, each according to the power of the wind, and the power of the lights of the moon, and according to the power that is fitting: and the divisions of the stars according to their names, and how all the divisions are divided. 13. And the thunders according to the places where they fall, and all the divisions that are made among the lightnings that it may lighten, and their host that they may at once obey. 14. For the thunder has †places of rest† (which) are assigned (to it) while it is waiting for its peal; and the thunder and lightning are inseparable, and although

not one and undivided, they both go together through the spirit and separate not.

15. For when the lightning lightens, the thunder utters its voice, and the spirit enforces a pause during the peal, and divides equally between them; for the treasury of their peals is like the sand, and each one of them as it peals is held in with a bridle, and turned back by the power of the spirit, and pushed forward according to the many quarters of the earth. And the spirit of the sea is masculine and strong, and according to the might of his strength he draws it back with a rein, and in like manner it is driven forward and disperses amid all the mountains of the earth. 17. And the spirit of the hoar-frost is his own angel, and the spirit of the hail is a good angel. 18. And the spirit of the snow has forsaken his chambers on account of his strength--There is a special spirit therein, and that which ascends from it is like smoke, and its name is frost. 19. And the spirit of the mist is not united with them in their chambers, but it has a special chamber; for its course is †glorious† both in light and in darkness, and in winter and in summer, and in its chamber is an angel. 20. And the spirit of the dew has its dwelling at the ends of the heaven, and is connected with the chambers of the rain, and its course is in winter and summer: and its clouds and the clouds of the mist are connected, and the one gives to the other. 21. And when the spirit of the rain goes forth from its chamber, the angels come and open the chamber and lead it out, and when it is diffused over the whole earth it unites with the water on the earth. And whensoever it unites with the water on the earth . . . 22. For the waters are for those who dwell on the earth; for they are nourishment for the earth from the Most High who is in heaven: therefore there is a measure for the rain, and the angels take it in charge. 23. And these things I saw towards the Garden of the Righteous. 24. And the angel of peace who was with me said to me: 'These two monsters, prepared conformably to the greatness of God, shall feed . . .

CHAPTER LXI.

1. And I saw in those days how long cords were given to those angels, and they took to themselves wings and flew, and they went towards the north.

2. And I asked the angel, saying unto him: 'Why have those (angels) taken these cords and gone off?' And he said unto me: 'They have gone to measure.'

3. And the angel who went with me said unto me:

'These shall bring the measures of the righteous,

And the ropes of the righteous to the righteous,

That they may stay themselves on the name of the Lord of Spirits for ever and ever.

4. The elect shall begin to dwell with the elect,

And those are the measures which
shall be given to faith And which shall
strengthen righteousness.

5. And these measures shall reveal all the secrets of the depths of the earth,

And those who have been destroyed by the desert,

And those who have been devoured by the beasts,

And those who have been devoured by the fish of the sea,

That they may return and stay themselves

On the day of the Elect One;

For none shall be destroyed before
the Lord of Spirits, And none can be
destroyed.

6. And all who dwell above in the heaven received a command and power and one voice and one light like unto fire.

7. And that One (with) their first words they blessed,

And extolled and lauded with wisdom,

And they were wise in utterance and in the spirit of life.

8. And the Lord of Spirits placed the Elect one on the throne of glory.

And he shall judge all the works of the holy
above in the heaven, And in the balance shall
their deeds be weighed

9. And when he shall lift up his countenance

To judge their secret ways according to the word of the name of the Lord of Spirits,

And their path according to the way of the righteous judgement of the Lord of Spirits,

Then shall they all with one voice speak and bless,

And glorify and extol and sanctify the name of the Lord of Spirits.

10. And He will summon all the host of the heavens, and all the holy ones above, and the host of God, the Cherubic, Seraphin and Ophannin, and all the angels of power, and all the angels of principalities, and the Elect One, and the other powers on the earth (and) over the water.

11. On that day shall raise one voice, and bless and glorify and exalt in the spirit of faith, and in the spirit of wisdom, and in the spirit of

patience, and in the spirit of mercy, and in the spirit of judgement and of peace, and in the spirit of goodness, and shall all say with one voice: "Blessed is He, and may the name of the Lord of Spirits be blessed for ever and ever."

12. All who sleep not above in heaven shall bless Him: All the holy ones who are in heaven shall bless Him, And all the elect who dwell in the garden of life:

And every spirit of light who is able to bless, and glorify, and extol, and hallow Thy blessed name,

And all flesh shall beyond measure glorify and bless Thy name for ever and ever.

13. For great is the mercy of the Lord of Spirits, and He is long-suffering,

And all His works and all that He has created He has revealed to the righteous and elect In the name of the Lord of Spirits.

CHAPTER LXII.

1. And thus the Lord commanded the kings and the mighty and the exalted, and those who dwell on the earth, and said: 'Open your eyes and lift up your horns if ye are able to recognize the Elect One.'

2. And the Lord of Spirits seated him on the throne of His glory,

And the spirit of righteousness was poured out upon him,

And the word of his mouth slays all the sinners,

And all the unrighteous are destroyed from before his face.

3. And there shall stand up in that day all the kings and the mighty,

And the exalted and those who hold the earth,

And they shall see and recognize How he sits on the throne of his glory, And righteousness is

judged before him, And no lying word is spoken
before him.

4. Then shall pain come upon them as on a woman in travail,

[And she has pain in bringing forth]

When her child enters the mouth of the womb, And she has pain in bringing forth.

5. And one portion of them shall look on the other,

And they shall be terrified,

And they shall be downcast of countenance,

And pain shall seize them,

When they see that Son of Man Sitting on the throne of his glory.

6. And the kings and the mighty and all who possess the earth shall bless and glorify and extol him who rules over all, who was hidden.

7. For from the beginning the Son of Man was hidden, And the Most High preserved him in the presence of His might, And revealed him to the elect.

8. And the congregation of the elect and holy shall be sown, And all the elect shall stand before him on that day.

9. And all the kings and the mighty and the exalted and those who rule the earth

Shall fall down before him on their faces,

And worship and set their hope upon that Son of Man, And petition him and supplicate for mercy at his hands.

10. Nevertheless that Lord of Spirits will so press them

That they shall hastily go forth from His presence, And their faces shall be filled with shame, And the darkness grow deeper on their faces.

11. And **He will deliver** them to the angels for punishment,

To execute vengeance on them because they have oppressed His children and His elect 12. And they shall be a spectacle for the righteous and for His elect:

They shall rejoice over them,

Because the wrath of the Lord of Spirits resteth upon them, And His sword is drunk with their blood.

13. And the righteous and elect shall be saved on that day,

And they shall never thenceforward see the face of the sinners and unrighteous.

14. And the Lord of Spirits will abide over them, And with that Son of Man shall they eat And lie down and rise up for ever and ever.

15. And the righteous and elect shall have risen from the earth, And ceased to be of downcast countenance.

And they shall have been clothed with garments of glory,

16. And these shall be the garments of life from the Lord of Spirits:

And your garments shall not grow old,

Nor your glory pass away before the Lord of Spirits.

CHAPTER LXIII.

1. In those days shall the mighty and the kings who possess the earth implore (Him) to grant them a little respite from His angels of punishment to whom they were delivered, that they might fall down and worship before the Lord of Spirits, and confess their sins before Him. 2. And they shall bless and glorify the Lord of Spirits, and say:

'Blessed is the Lord of Spirits and the Lord of kings,

And the Lord of the mighty and the Lord of the rich,

And the Lord of glory and the Lord of wisdom,

3. And splendid in every secret thing is Thy power from generation to generation, And Thy glory for ever and ever:

Deep are all Thy secrets and innumerable, And Thy righteousness is beyond reckoning.

4. We have now learnt that we should glorify

And bless the Lord of kings and Him who is king over all kings.' 5. And they shall say:

'Would that we had rest to glorify and give thanks And confess our faith before His glory!

6. And now we long for a little rest but find it not: We follow hard upon and obtain (it) not:

And light has vanished from before us,

And darkness is our dwelling-place for ever and ever:

7. For we have not believed before Him

Nor glorified the name of the Lord of Spirits, [nor glorified our Lord]

But our hope was in the sceptre of our kingdom, And in our glory.

8. And in the day of our suffering and tribulation He saves us not, And we find no respite for confession

That our Lord is true in all His works, and in His judgements and His justice, And His judgements have no respect of persons.

9. And we pass away from before His face on account of our works, And all our sins are reckoned up in righteousness.'

10. Now they shall say unto themselves: 'Our souls are full of unrighteous gain, but it does not prevent us from descending from the midst thereof into the †burden† of Sheol.'

11. And after that their faces shall be filled with darkness

And shame before that Son of Man,

And they shall be driven from his presence,

And the sword shall abide before his face in their midst.

12. Thus spake the Lord of Spirits: 'This is the ordinance and judgement with respect to the mighty and the kings and the exalted and those who possess the earth before the Lord of Spirits.'

CHAPTER LXIV.

1. And other forms I saw hidden in that place. 2. I heard the voice of the angel saying: 'These are the angels who descended to the earth, and revealed what was hidden to the children of men and seduced the children of men into committing sin.'

CHAPTER LXV.

1. And in those days Noah saw the earth that it had sunk down and its destruction was nigh. 2. And he arose from thence and went to the ends of the earth, and cried aloud to his grandfather Enoch: and Noah said three times with an embittered voice: Hear me, hear me, hear me.' 3. And I said unto him: 'Tell me what it is that is falling out on the earth that the earth is in such evil plight and shaken, lest perchance I shall perish with it?' 4. And thereupon there was a great commotion, on the earth, and a voice was heard from heaven, and I fell on my face. 5. And Enoch my grandfather came and stood by me, and said unto me: 'Why hast thou cried unto me with a bitter cry and weeping?

6. And a command has gone forth from the presence of the Lord concerning those who dwell on the earth that their ruin is accomplished because they have learnt all the secrets of the angels, and all the violence of the Satans, and all their powers--the most secret ones--and all the power of those who practice sorcery, and the power of witchcraft, and the power of those who make molten images for the whole earth: 7. And how silver is produced from the dust of the earth, and how soft metal originates in the earth. 8. For lead and tin are not produced from the earth like the first: it is a fountain that produces them, and an angel stands therein, and that angel is pre-eminent.' 9. And after that my grandfather Enoch took hold of me by my hand and raised me up, and said unto me: 'Go, for I have asked the Lord of Spirits as touching this commotion on the earth. 10. And He said unto me: "Because of their

unrighteousness their judgement has been determined upon and shall not be **withheld** by Me for ever. Because of the **sorceries** which they have searched out and learnt, the earth and those who dwell upon it shall be destroyed." 11. And these--they have no **place of repentance** for ever, because they have shown them what was hidden, and they are the damned: but as for thee, my son, the Lord of Spirits knows that thou art pure, and guiltless of this reproach concerning the secrets.

12. And He has destined thy name to be among the holy,

And will preserve thee amongst those who dwell on the earth,

And has destined thy righteous seed both for kingship and for great honours,

And from thy seed shall proceed a fountain of the righteous and holy without number for ever.

CHAPTER LXVI.

1. And after that he showed me the angels of punishment who are prepared to come and let loose all the powers of the waters which are beneath in the earth in order to bring judgement and destruction on all who [abide and] dwell on the earth. 2. And the Lord of Spirits gave commandment to the angels who were going forth, that they should not cause **the waters** to rise but should hold them in check; for those angels were over the powers of the waters. 3.

And I went away from the presence of Enoch.

CHAPTER LXVII.

1. And in those days the word of God came unto me, and He said unto me: 'Noah, thy lot has come up before Me, a lot without blame, a lot of love and uprightness. 2. And now the angels are making a wooden (building),

and when they have completed that task I will place My hand upon it and preserve it, and there shall come forth from it the seed of life, and a change shall set in so that the earth will not remain without inhabitant. 3. And I will make fast thy seed before me for ever and ever, and I will spread abroad those who dwell with thee: it shall not **be unfruitful** on the face of the earth, but it shall be blessed and multiply on the earth in the name of the Lord.'

4. And He will imprison those angels, who have shown unrighteousness, in that burning valley which my grandfather Enoch had formerly shown to me in the west among the mountains of gold and silver and iron and soft metal and tin. 5. And I saw that valley in which there was a great convulsion and a convulsion of the waters. 6. And when all this took place, from that fiery molten metal and from the convulsion thereof in that place, there was produced a smell of sulphur, and it was connected with those waters, and that valley of the angels who had led astray (mankind) burned beneath that land. 7. And through its valleys proceed streams of fire, where these angels are punished who had led astray those who dwell upon the earth.

8. But those waters shall in those days serve for the kings and the mighty and the exalted, and those who dwell on the earth, for the healing of the body, but for the punishment of the spirit; now their spirit is full of lust, that they may be punished in their body, for they have denied the Lord of Spirits and see their punishment daily, and yet believe not in His name. 9. And in proportion as the burning of their bodies becomes severe, a corresponding change shall take place in their spirit for ever and ever; for before the Lord of Spirits none shall utter an idle word. 10. For the judgement shall come upon them, because they believe in the lust of their body and deny the Spirit of the Lord. 11. And those same waters will undergo a change in those days; for when those angels are punished in these waters, these water-springs shall change their temperature, and

when the angels ascend, this water of the springs shall change and become cold. 12. And I heard Michael answering and saying: 'This judgement wherewith the angels are judged is a testimony for the kings and the mighty who possess the earth.' 13. Because these waters of judgement minister to the healing of the body of the **kings** and the lust of their body; therefore they will not see and will not believe that those waters will change and become a fire which burns for ever.

CHAPTER LXVIII.

1. And after that my grandfather Enoch gave me the teaching of all the secrets in the book in the Parables which had been given to him, and he put them together for me in the words of the book of the Parables. 2. And on that day Michael answered Raphael and said: 'The power of the spirit transports and **makes me to tremble** because of the severity of the judgement of the secrets, the judgement of the angels: who can endure the severe judgement which has been executed, and before which they melt away?' 3. And Michael answered again, and said to Raphael: 'Who is he whose heart is not softened concerning it, and whose reins are not troubled by this word of judgement (that) has gone forth upon them because of those who have thus led them out?' 4. And it came to pass when he stood before the Lord of Spirits, Michael said thus to Raphael: 'I will not take their part under the eye of the Lord; for the Lord of Spirits has been angry with them because they do as if they were the Lord. Therefore all that is hidden shall come upon them for ever and ever; for neither angel nor man shall have his portion (in it), but alone they have received their judgement for ever and ever.'

CHAPTER LXIX.

1 And after this judgement they shall terrify and **make** them **to tremble** because they have shown this to those who dwell on the earth.

2 And behold the names of those angels [and these are their names: the first of them is Samjâzâ, the second Artâqîfâ, and the third Armên, the fourth Kôkabêl, the fifth †Tûrâêl†, the sixth Rûmjâl, the seventh Dânjâl, the eighth †Nêqâêl†, the ninth Barâqêl, the tenth

Azâzêl, the eleventh Armârôs, the twelfth Batarjâl, the thirteenth †Busasêjal†, the fourteenth Hanânêl, the fifteenth †Tûrêl†, and the sixteenth Sîmâpêsîêl, the seventeenth Jetrêl, the eighteenth Tûmâêl, the nineteenth Tûrêl, the twentieth †Rumâêl†, the twenty-first †Azâzêl†.

3. And these are the chiefs of their angels and their names, and their chief ones over hundreds and over fifties and over tens].

4. The name of the first Jeqôn: that is, the one who led astray [all] the sons of **God**, and brought them down to the earth, and led them astray through the daughters of men. 5. And the second was named Asbeêl: he imparted to the holy sons of **God** evil counsel, and led them astray so that they defiled their bodies with the daughters of men. 6. And the third was named Gâdreêl: he it is who showed the children of men all the blows of death, and he led astray

Eve, and showed [the weapons of death to the sons of men] the shield and the coat of mail, and the sword for battle, and all the weapons of death to the children of men. 7. And from his hand they have proceeded against those who dwell on the earth from that day and for evermore. 8. And the fourth was named Pênêmûe: he taught the children of men the bitter and the sweet, and he taught them all the secrets of their wisdom. 9. And he instructed mankind in writing with ink and paper, and thereby many sinned from eternity to eternity and until this day. 10. For men were not created for such a purpose, to give confirmation to their good faith with pen and ink. 11. For men were created exactly like the angels, to the intent that they should continue pure and righteous, and death, which destroys everything, could not have taken hold of them, but through this their knowledge they are perishing, and through this power it is consuming me†. 12. And the fifth was named Kâsdejâ: this is he who showed the children of men all the wicked smitings of spirits and demons, and the smitings of the embryo in the womb, that it may pass away, and [the smitings of the soul] the bites of the serpent, and the smitings which befall through the noontide heat, the son of the serpent named Tabââ'ĕt. 13. And this is the **task** of Kâsbeêl, the chief of the oath which he showed to the holy ones when he dwelt high above in glory, and its name is Bîqâ. 14. This (angel) requested Michael to show him the hidden name, that he might enunciate it in the oath, so that those might quake before that name and oath who revealed all that was in secret to the children of men. 15. And this is the power of this oath, for it is powerful and strong, and he placed this oath Akâe in the hand of Michael. 16 And these are the secrets of this oath . . .

And they are strong through his oath:

And the heaven was suspended before the
world was created, And for ever.

17. And through it the earth was founded upon the water,

And from the secret recesses of the mountains come
beautiful waters, From the creation of the world and
unto eternity.

18. And through that oath the sea was created,

And †as its foundation† He set for it the sand against the
time of (its) anger, And it dare not pass beyond it from the
creation of the world unto eternity.

19. And through that oath are the depths made fast,

And abide and stir not from their place from eternity to eternity.

20. And through that oath the sun and moon complete their course, And deviate not from their ordinance from eternity to eternity.

21. And through that oath the stars complete their course,

And He calls them by their names,

And they answer Him from eternity to eternity.

[22. And in like manner the spirits of the water, and of the winds, and of all zephyrs, and (their) paths from all the quarters of the winds. 23. And there are preserved the voices of the thunder and the light of the lightnings: and there are preserved the chambers of the hail and the chambers of the hoarfrost, and the chambers of the mist, and the chambers of the rain and the dew. 24. And all these believe and give thanks before the Lord of Spirits, and glorify (Him) with all their power, and their food is in every act of thanksgiving: they thank and glorify and extol the name of the Lord of Spirits for ever and ever.]

25. And this oath is mighty over them

And through it [they are preserved and] their paths are preserved, And their course is not destroyed.

Close of the Third Parable.

26. And there was great joy amongst them,

And they blessed and glorified and extolled

Because the name of that Son of Man had been revealed unto them.

27. And he sat on the throne of his glory,

And the sum of judgement was given unto the Son of Man,

And he caused the sinners to pass away and be destroyed from off the face of the earth, And those who have led the world astray.

28. With chains shall they be bound,

And in their assemblage-place of destruction shall they be imprisoned, And all their works vanish from the face of the earth.

29. And from henceforth there shall be nothing corruptible;

For that Son of Man has appeared,

And has seated himself on the throne of his glory,

And all evil shall pass away before his face, And the word of that Son of Man shall go forth And be strong before the Lord of Spirits.

CHAPTER LXX.

1. And it came to pass after this that his name during his lifetime was raised aloft to that Son of Man and to the Lord of Spirits from amongst those who dwell on the earth. 2. And he was raised aloft on the chariots of the spirit and his name vanished among them. 3. And from that day I was no longer numbered amongst them: and he set me between the two winds, between the North and the West, where the angels took the cords to measure for me the place for the elect and righteous. 4. And there I saw the first fathers and the righteous who from the beginning dwell in that place.

CHAPTER LXXI.

1. And it came to pass after this that my spirit was translated And it ascended into the heavens: And I saw the **holy sons of God**.

They were stepping on flames of fire: Their garments were white [and their raiment], And their faces shone like snow.

2. And I saw two streams of fire,

And the light of that fire shone like hyacinth, And I fell on my face before the Lord of Spirits.

3. And the angel Michael [one of the archangels] seized me by my right hand, And lifted me up and led me forth into all the secrets, And he showed me all the secrets of righteousness.

4. And he showed me all the secrets of the ends of the heaven, And all the chambers of all the stars, and all the luminaries, Whence they proceed before the face of the holy ones.

5. And he translated my spirit into the heaven of heavens, And I saw there as it were a structure built of crystals, And between those crystals tongues of living fire.

6. And my spirit saw the girdle which girt that house of fire, And on its four sides were streams full of living fire, And they girt that house.

7. And round about were Seraphin, Cherubic, and Ophannin: And these are they who sleep not And guard the throne of His glory.

8. And I saw angels who could not be counted,

A thousand thousands, and ten thousand times ten thousand, Encircling that house.

And Michael, and Raphael, and Gabriel, and Phanuel, And the holy angels who are above the heavens, Go in and out of that house.

9. And they came forth from that house,

And Michael and Gabriel, Raphael and Phanuel, And many holy angels without number.

10. And with them the Head of Days, His head white and pure as wool, And His raiment indescribable.

11. And I fell on my face,

And my whole body became relaxed, And my spirit was transfigured;

And I cried with a loud voice,

. . .with the spirit of power,

And blessed and glorified and extolled.

12. And these blessings which went forth out of my mouth were well pleasing before that Head of Days. 13. And that Head of Days came with Michael and Gabriel, Raphael and Phanuel, thousands and ten thousands of angels without number.

[Lost passage wherein the Son of Man was described as accompanying the Head of Days, and Enoch asked one of the angels (as in 46) concerning the Son of Man as to who he was.]

14. And he (*i.e.* the angel) came to me and greeted me with His voice, and said unto me:

'**This is** the Son of Man who is born unto righteousness;

And righteousness abides over him,

And the righteousness of the Head of Days forsakes him not.' 15. And he said unto me:

'He proclaims unto thee peace in the name of the world to come; For from hence has proceeded peace since the creation of the world, And so shall it be unto thee for ever and for ever and ever.

16. And all shall walk in **his** ways since righteousness never forsaketh **him**: With **him** will be their dwelling-places, and with **him** their

heritage, And they shall not be separated from him for ever and ever and ever.

17. And so there shall be length of days with that Son of Man,

And the righteous shall have peace and an upright way

In the name of the Lord of Spirits for ever and ever.'

The Book Of The Courses Of The Heavenly Luminaries

CHAPTER LXXII.

1. The book of the courses of the luminaries of the heaven, the relations of each, according to their classes, their dominion and their seasons, according to their names and places of origin, and according to their months, which Uriel, the holy angel, who was with me, who is their guide, showed me; and he showed me all their laws exactly as they are, and how it is with regard to all the years of the world and unto eternity, till the new creation is accomplished which dureth till eternity. 2. And this is the first law of the luminaries: the luminary the Sun has its rising in the eastern portals of the heaven, and its setting in the western portals of the heaven. 3. And I saw six portals in which the sun rises, and six portals in which the sun sets and the moon rises and sets in these portals, and the leaders of the stars and those whom they lead: six in the east and six in the west, and all following each other in accurately corresponding order: also many windows to the right and left of these portals. 4. And first there goes forth the great luminary, named the Sun, and his circumference is like the circumference of the heaven, and he is quite filled with illuminating and heating fire. 5. The chariot on which he ascends, the wind drives, and the sun goes down from the heaven and

returns through the north in order to reach the east, and is so guided that he comes to the appropriate (lit. 'that') portal and shines in the face of the heaven. 6. In this way he rises in the first month in the great portal, which is the fourth [those six portals in the cast]. 7. And in that fourth portal from which the sun rises in the first month are twelve window-openings, from which proceed a flame when they are opened in their season. 8. When the sun rises in the heaven, he comes forth through that fourth portal thirty mornings in succession, and sets accurately in the fourth portal in the west of the heaven. 9. And during this period the day becomes daily longer and the night nightly shorter to the thirtieth morning. 10. On that day the day is longer than the night by a ninth part, and the day amounts exactly to ten parts and the night to eight parts. 11. And the sun rises from that fourth portal, and sets in the fourth and returns to the fifth portal of the east thirty mornings, and rises from it and sets in the fifth portal. 12. And then the day becomes longer by †two† parts and amounts to eleven parts, and the night becomes shorter and amounts to seven parts. 13. And it returns to the east and enters into the sixth portal, and rises and sets in the sixth portal one-and-thirty mornings on account of its sign. 14. On that day the day becomes longer than the night, and the day becomes double the night, and the day becomes twelve parts, and the night is shortened and becomes six parts. 15. And the sun mounts up to make the day shorter and the night longer, and the sun returns to the east and enters into the sixth portal, and rises from it and sets thirty mornings. 16. And when thirty mornings are accomplished, the day decreases by exactly one part, and becomes eleven parts, and the night seven. 17. And the sun goes forth from that sixth portal in the west, and goes to the east and rises in the fifth portal for thirty mornings, and sets in the west again in the fifth western portal. 18. On that day the day decreases by †two† parts, and amounts to ten parts and the night to eight parts. 19. And the sun goes forth from that fifth portal and sets in the fifth portal of the west, and rises in the fourth portal for one-and-thirty mornings on account of its sign, and sets in the west. 20. On that day the day is equalized with the night, [and becomes of equal length], and the night amounts to nine parts and the day to nine parts. 21. And the sun rises from that portal and sets in the west, and returns to the east and rises thirty mornings in the third portal and sets in the west in the third portal. 22. And on that day the night becomes longer than the day, and night becomes longer than night, and day shorter than day till the thirtieth morning, and the night amounts exactly to ten parts and the day to eight parts. 23. And the sun rises from that third portal and sets in the third portal in the west and returns to the east, and for thirty mornings rises in the second portal in the east, and in like manner sets in the second portal in the west of the heaven. 24. And on that day the night amounts to eleven parts and the day to seven parts. 25. And the sun rises on that day from that second portal and sets in the west in the second portal, and returns to the east into the first portal for one-and-thirty mornings, and sets in the first portal in the west of the heaven. 26. And on that day the night becomes longer and amounts to the double of the day: and the night amounts exactly to twelve parts and the day to six. 27. And the sun has (therewith) traversed the divisions of his orbit and turns again on those divisions of his orbit, and enters that portal thirty mornings and sets also in the west opposite to it. 28. And on that night has the night decreased in length by a †ninth† part, and the night has become eleven parts and the day seven parts. 29. And the sun has returned and entered into the second portal in the east, and returns on those his divisions of his orbit for thirty mornings, rising and setting. 30. And on that day the night decreases in length, and the night amounts to ten parts and the day to eight. 31. And on that day the sun rises from that portal, and sets in the west, and returns to the east, and rises in the third portal for one-and-thirty mornings, and sets in the west of the heaven. 32. On that day the night decreases and amounts to nine parts, and the day to nine parts, and the night is equal to the day and the year is exactly as to its days three hundred and sixty-four. 33. And the length of the day and of the night, and the shortness of the day and of the night arise--through the course of the sun these distinctions are made (lit. 'they are separated'). 34. So it comes that its course becomes daily longer, and its course nightly shorter. 35. And this is the law and the course of the sun, and his return as often as he returns sixty times and rises, *i.e.* the great luminary which is named the sun, for ever and ever. 36. And that which (thus) rises is the great luminary, and is so named according to its appearance, according as the Lord commanded. 37. As he rises, so he sets and decreases not, and rests not, but runs day and night, and his light is sevenfold brighter than that of the moon; but as regards size they are both equal.

CHAPTER LXXIII.

1. And after this law I saw another law dealing with the smaller luminary, which is named the Moon. 2. And her circumference is like the circumference of the heaven, and her chariot in which she rides is driven by the wind, and light is given to her in (definite) measure. 3. And her rising and setting change every month: and her days are like the days of the sun, and when her light is uniform (*i.e.* full) it amounts to the seventh part of the light of the sun. 4. And thus she rises. And her first phase in the east comes forth on the thirtieth morning: and on that day she becomes visible, and constitutes for you the first phase of the moon on the thirtieth day together with the sun in the portal where the sun rises. 5. And the one half of her goes forth by a seventh part, and her whole circumference is empty, without light, with the exception of one-seventh part of it, (and) the fourteenth part of her light. 6. And when she receives one-seventh part of the half of her light, her light amounts to one-seventh part and the half thereof. 7. And she sets with the sun, and when the sun rises the moon rises with him and receives the half of one part of light, and in that night in the beginning of her morning [in the

commencement of the lunar day] the moon sets with the sun, and is invisible that night with the fourteen parts and the half of one of them. 8. And she rises on that day with exactly a seventh part, and comes forth and recedes from the rising of the sun, and in her remaining days she becomes bright in the (remaining) thirteen parts.

CHAPTER LXXIV.

1. And I saw another course, a law for her, (and) how according to that law she performs her monthly revolution. 2. And all these Uriel, the holy angel who is the leader of them all, showed to me, and their positions, and I wrote down their positions as he showed them to me, and I wrote down their months as they were, and the appearance of their lights till fifteen days were accomplished. 3. In single seventh parts she accomplishes all her light in the east, and in single seventh parts accomplishes all her darkness in the west. 4. And in certain months she alters her settings, and in certain months she pursues her own peculiar course. 5. In two months the moon sets with the sun: in those two middle portals the third and the fourth. 6. She goes forth for seven days, and turns about and returns again through the portal where the sun rises, and accomplishes all her light: and she recedes from the sun, and in eight days enters the sixth portal from which the sun goes forth. 7. And when the sun goes forth from the fourth portal she goes forth seven days, until she goes forth from the fifth and turns back again in seven days into the fourth portal and accomplishes all her light: and she recedes and enters into the first portal in eight days. 8. And she returns again in seven days into the fourth portal from which the sun goes forth. 9. Thus I saw their position--how the moons rose and the sun set in those days. 10. And if five years are added together the sun has an overplus of thirty days, and all the days which accrue to it for one of those five years, when they are full, amount to 364 days. 11. And the overplus of the sun and of the stars amounts to six days: in 5 years 6 days every year come to 30 days: and the

moon falls behind the sun and stars to the number of 30 days. 12. And **the sun** and the stars bring in all the years exactly, so that they do not advance or delay their position by a single day unto eternity; but **complete** the years with perfect justice in 364 days. 13. In 3 years there are 1092 days, and in 5 years 1820 days, so that in 8 years there are 2912 days. 14. For the moon alone the days amount in 3 years to 1062 days, and in 5 years she falls 50 days behind: [*i.e.* to the sum (of 1770) there is to be added (1000 and) 62 days.] 15. And in 5 years there are 1770 days, so that for the moon the days in 8 years amount to 2832 days. 16. [For in 8 years she falls behind to the amount of 80 days], all the days she falls behind in 8 years are 80. 17. And the year is accurately completed in conformity with their world-stations and the stations of the sun, which rise from the portals through which it (the sun) rises and sets 30 days.

CHAPTER LXXV.

1. And the leaders of the heads of the thousands, who are placed over the whole creation and over all the stars, have also to do with the four intercalary days, being inseparable from their office, according to the reckoning of the year, and these render service on the four days which are not reckoned in the reckoning of the year. 2. And owing to them men go wrong therein, for those luminaries truly render service on the world-stations, one in the first portal, one in the third portal of the heaven, one in the fourth portal, and one in the sixth portal, and the exactness of the year is accomplished through its separate three hundred and sixty-four stations. 3. For the signs and the times and the years and the days the angel Uriel showed to me, whom the Lord of glory hath set for ever over all the luminaries of the heaven, in the heaven and in the world, that they should rule on the face of the heaven and be seen on the earth, and be leaders for the day and the night, *i.e.* the sun, moon, and stars, and all the ministering creatures which make their revolution in all the chariots of the heaven. 4. In like manner twelve doors Uriel showed me, open in

the circumference of the sun's chariot in the heaven, through which the rays of the sun break forth: and from them is warmth diffused over the earth, when they are opened at their appointed seasons. 5. [And for the winds and the spirit of the dew† when they are opened, standing open in the heavens at the ends.] 6. As for the twelve portals in the heaven, at the ends of the earth, out of which go forth the sun, moon, and stars, and all the works of heaven in the east and in the west. 7. There are many windows open to the left and right of them, and one window at its (appointed) season produces

warmth, corresponding (as these do) to those doors from which the stars come forth according as He has commanded them, and wherein they set corresponding to their number. 8. And I saw chariots in the heaven, running in the world, above those portals in which revolve the stars that never set. 9. And one is larger than all the rest, and it is that that makes its course through the entire world.

CHAPTER LXXVI.

1 And at the ends of the earth I saw twelve portals open to all the **quarters** (of the heaven), from which the winds go forth and blow over the earth. 2. Three of them are open on the face (*i.e.* the east) of the heavens, and three in the west, and three on the right (*i.e.* the south) of the heaven, and three on the left (*i.e.* the north). 3. And the three first are those of the east, and three are of †the north, and three [after those on the left] of the south†, and three of the west. 4. Through four of these come winds of blessing and prosperity, and from those eight come hurtful winds: when they are sent, they bring destruction on all the earth and on the water upon it, and on all who dwell thereon, and on everything which is in the water and on the land.

5. And the first wind from those portals, called the east wind, comes forth through the first portal which is in the east, inclining towards the south: from it come forth desolation, drought, heat, and destruction. 6. And through the second portal in the middle comes what is fitting, and from it there come rain and fruitfulness and prosperity and dew; and through the third portal which lies toward the north come cold and drought.

7. And after these come forth the south winds through three portals: through the first portal of them inclining to the east comes forth a hot wind. 8. And through the middle portal next to it there come forth fragrant smells, and dew and rain, and prosperity and health. 9. And through the third portal lying to the west come forth dew and rain, locusts and desolation.

10. And after these the north winds: from the seventh portal in the east come dew and rain, locusts and desolation. 11. And from the middle portal come in a direct direction health and rain and dew and prosperity; and through the third portal in the west come cloud and hoarfrost, and snow and rain, and dew and locusts.

12. And after these [four] are the west winds: through the first portal adjoining the north come forth dew and hoar-frost, and cold and snow and frost. And from the middle portal come forth dew and rain, and prosperity and blessing; and through the last portal which adjoins the south come forth drought and desolation, and burning and destruction. 14. And the twelve portals of the four **quarters** of the heaven are therewith completed, and all their laws and all their plagues and all their benefactions have I shown to thee, my son Methuselah.

CHAPTER LXXVII.

1. And the first **quarter** is called the east, because it is the first: and the second, the south, because the Most High **will descend** there, yea, there

in quite a special sense will He who is blessed for ever **descend.** 2. And the west **quarter** is named the diminished, because there all the luminaries of the heaven wane and go down. 3. And the fourth **quarter**, named the north, is divided into three parts: the first of them is for the dwelling of men: and the second contains seas of water, and the abysses and forests and rivers, and darkness and clouds; and the third part contains the garden of righteousness.

4. I saw seven high mountains, higher than all the mountains which are on the earth: and thence comes forth hoar-frost, and days, seasons, and years pass away. 5. I saw seven rivers on the earth larger than all the rivers: one of them coming from the west pours its waters into the Great Sea. 6. And these two come from the north to the sea and pour their waters into the Erythraean Sea in the east. 7. And the remaining four come forth on the side of the north to their own sea, ⟨two of them⟩ to the Erythraean Sea, and two into the Great Sea and discharge themselves there [and some say: into the desert]. 8. Seven great islands I saw in the sea and in the mainland: two in the mainland and five in the Great Sea.

CHAPTER LXXVII.

1. And the names of the sun are the following: the first Orjârês, and the second Tômâs. 2. And the moon has four names: the first name is Asônjâ, the second Eblâ, the third Benâsê, and the fourth Erâe. 3. These are the two great luminaries: their circumference is like the circumference of the heaven, and the size of the circumference of both is alike. 4. In the circumference of the sun there are seven portions of light which are added to it more than to the moon, and in definite measures it is s transferred till the seventh portion of the sun is exhausted. 5. And they set and enter the portals of the west, and make their revolution by the north, and come forth through the eastern portals on the face of the heaven. 6. And when the moon rises one-fourteenth part appears in the

heaven: [the light becomes full in her]: on the fourteenth day she accomplishes her light. 7. And fifteen parts of light are transferred to her till the fifteenth day (when) her light is accomplished, according to the sign of the year, and she becomes fifteen parts, and the moon grows by (the addition of) fourteenth parts. 8. And in her waning (the moon) decreases on the first day to fourteen parts of her light, on the second to thirteen parts of light, on the third to twelve, on the fourth to eleven, on the fifth to ten, on the sixth to nine, on the seventh to eight, on the eighth to seven, on the ninth to six, on the tenth to five, on the eleventh to four, on the twelfth to three, on the thirteenth to two, on the fourteenth to the half of a seventh, and all her remaining light disappears wholly on the fifteenth. 9. And in certain months the month has twenty-nine days and once twenty-eight.

10. And Uriel showed me another law: when light is transferred to the moon, and on which side it is transferred to her by the sun. 11. During all the period during which the moon is growing in her light, she is transferring it to herself when opposite to the sun during fourteen days [her light is accomplished in the heaven], and when she is illumined throughout, her light is accomplished full in the heaven. 12. And on the first day she is called the new moon, for on that day the light rises upon her. 13. She becomes full moon exactly on the day when the sun sets in the west, and from the east she rises at night, and the moon shines the whole night through till the sun rises over against her and the moon is seen over against the sun. 14. On the side whence the light of the moon comes forth, there again she wanes till all the light vanishes and all the days of the month are at an end, and her circumference is empty, void of light. 15. And three months she makes of thirty days, and at her time she makes three months of twenty-nine days each, in which she accomplishes her waning in the first period of time, and in the first portal for one hundred and seventy-seven days. 16. And in the time of her going out she appears for three months (of) thirty days each, and for three

months she appears (of) twenty-nine each. 17. At night she appears like a man for twenty days each time, and by day she appears like the heaven, and there is nothing else in her save her light.

CHAPTER LXXIX.

1. And now, my son, I have shown thee everything, and the law of all the stars of the heaven is completed. 2. And he showed me all the laws of these for every day, and for every season of bearing rule, and for every year, and for its going forth, and for the order prescribed to it every month and every week: 3. And the waning of the moon which takes place in the sixth portal: for in this sixth portal her light is accomplished, and after that there is the beginning of the waning: 4. ⟨And the waning⟩ which takes place in the first portal in its season, till one hundred and seventy-seven days are accomplished: reckoned according to weeks, twenty-five (weeks) and two days. 5. She falls behind the sun and the order of the stars exactly five days in the course of one period, and when this place which thou seest has been traversed. 6. Such is the picture and sketch of every luminary which Uriel the archangel, who is their leader, showed unto me.

CHAPTER LXXX.

1. And in those days the angel Uriel answered and said to me: 'Behold, I have shown thee everything, Enoch, and I have revealed everything to thee that thou shouldst see this sun and this moon, and the leaders of the stars of the heaven and all those who turn them, their tasks and times and departures.

2. And in the days of the sinners the years shall be shortened,

And their seed shall be tardy on their lands and fields, And all things on the earth shall alter, And shall not appear in their time: And the rain shall be kept back And the heaven shall withhold (it).

3. And in those times the fruits of the earth shall be backward,

And shall not grow in their time,

And the fruits of the trees shall be withheld in their time.

4. And the moon shall alter her order, And not appear at her time.

5. [And in those days the **sun** shall be seen and he shall journey in the **evening** †on the extremity of the great chariot† in the west]

And shall shine more brightly than accords with the order of light.

6. And many chiefs of the stars shall transgress the order (prescribed). And these shall alter their orbits and tasks,

And not appear at the seasons prescribed to them.

7. And the whole order of the stars shall be concealed from the sinners,

And the thoughts of those on the earth shall err concerning them, [And they shall be altered from all their ways], Yea, they shall err and take them to be gods.

8. And evil shall be multiplied upon them,

And punishment shall come upon them So as to destroy all.'

CHAPTER LXXXI.

1. And he said unto me:

'Observe, Enoch, these heavenly tablets,

And read what is written thereon, And mark every individual fact.'

2 And I observed the heavenly tablets, and read everything which was written (thereon) and understood everything, and read the book of all the deeds of mankind, and of all the children of flesh that shall be upon

the earth to the remotest generations. 3. And forthwith I blessed the great Lord the King of glory for ever, in that He has made all the works of the world,

And I extolled the Lord because of His patience, And blessed Him because of the children of men.

4. And after that I said:

'Blessed is the man who dies in righteousness and goodness,

Concerning whom there is no book of unrighteousness written, And against whom no day of judgement shall be found.'

5. And those seven holy ones brought me and placed me on the earth before the door of my house, and said to me: 'Declare everything to thy son Methuselah, and show to all thy children that no flesh is righteous in the sight of the Lord, for He is their Creator. 6. One year we will leave thee with thy son, till thou givest thy (last) commands, that thou mayest teach thy children and record (it) for them, and testify to all thy children; and in the second year they shall take thee from their midst.

7. Let thy heart be strong,

For the good shall announce righteousness to the good;

The righteous with the righteous shall rejoice, And shall offer congratulation to one another.

8. But the sinners shall die with the sinners, And the apostate go down with the apostate.

9. And those who practice righteousness shall die on account of the deeds of men, And be taken away on account of the doings of the godless.'

10. And in those days they ceased to speak to me, and I came to my people, blessing the Lord of the world.

CHAPTER LXXXII.

1. And now, my son Methuselah, all these things I am recounting to thee and writing down for thee, and I have revealed to thee everything, and given thee books concerning all these: so preserve, my son Methuselah, the books from thy father's hand, and (see) that thou deliver them to the generations of the world.

2. I have given Wisdom to thee and to thy children,

[And thy children that shall be to thee],

That they may give it to their children for generations, This wisdom (namely) that passeth their thought.

3. And those who understand it shall not sleep,

But shall listen with the ear that they may learn this wisdom, And it shall please those that eat thereof better than good food.

4. Blessed are all the righteous, blessed are all those who walk in the way of righteousness and sin not as the sinners, in the reckoning of all their days in which the sun traverses the heaven, entering into and departing from the portals for thirty days with the heads of thousands of the order of the stars, together with the four which are intercalated which divide the four portions of the year, which lead them and enter with them four days. 5. Owing to them men shall be at fault and not reckon them in the **whole reckoning of the year**: yea, men shall be at fault, and not recognize them accurately. 6. For they belong to the reckoning of the year and are truly recorded (thereon) for ever, one in the first portal and one in the third, and one in the fourth and one in the sixth, and the year is completed in three hundred and sixtyfour days.

7. And the account thereof is accurate and the recorded reckoning thereof exact; for the luminaries, and months and festivals, and years and

days, has Uriel shown and revealed to me, **to whom** the Lord of the whole creation of the world hath **subjected** the host of heaven.

8. And he has power over night and day in the heaven to cause the light to give light to men-sun, moon, and stars, and all the powers of the heaven which revolve in their circular chariots. 9. And these are the orders of the stars, which set in their places, and in their seasons and festivals and months. 10. And these are the names of those who lead them, who watch that they enter at their times, in their orders, in their seasons, in their months, in their periods of dominion, and in their positions. 11. Their four leaders who divide the four parts of the year enter first; and after them the twelve leaders of the orders who divide the months; and for the three hundred and sixty (days) there are heads over thousands who divide the days; and for the four intercalary days there are the leaders which sunder the four parts of the year.

12. And these heads over thousands are intercalated between leader and leader, each behind a station, but their leaders make the division. And these are the names of the leaders who divide the four parts of the year which are ordained: Mîlkî'êl, Hel'emmêlêk, and Mêl'êjal, and Nârêl. 13. And the names of those who lead them: Adnâr'êl, and Îjâsûsa'êl, and 'Elômê'êl-these three follow the leaders of the orders, and there is one that follows the three leaders of the orders which follow those leaders of stations that divide the four parts of the year.

15. In the beginning of the year Melkejâl rises first and rules, who is named †Tam'âinî† and sun, and all the days of his dominion whilst he bears rule are ninety-one days. 16. And these are the signs of the days which are to be seen on earth in the days of his dominion: sweat, and heat, and calms; and all the trees bear fruit, and leaves are produced on all the trees, and the harvest of wheat, and the rose-flowers, and all the flowers which come forth in the field, but the trees of the winter season become withered. 17. And these are the names of the leaders which are under them: Berka'êl, Zêlebs'êl, and another who is added a head of a thousand, called Hîlûjâsĕph: and the days of the dominion of this (leader)

are at an end. 18. The next leader after him is Hêl'emmêlêk, whom one names the shining sun, and all the days of his light are ninety-one days. 19. And these are the signs of (his) days on the earth: glowing heat and dryness, and the trees ripen their fruits and produce all their fruits ripe and ready, and the sheep pair and become pregnant, and all the fruits of the earth are gathered in, and everything that is in the fields, and the winepress: these things take place in the days of his dominion. 20. These are the names, and the orders, and the leaders of those heads of thousands: Gîdâ'îjal, Kê'êl, and Hê'êl, and the name of the head of a thousand which is added to them, Asfâ'êl': and the days of his dominion are at an end.

The Dream-Visions

CHAPTER LXXXIII.

1. And now, my son Methuselah, I will show thee all my visions which I have seen, recounting them before thee. 2. Two visions I saw before I took a wife, and the one was quite unlike the other: the first when I was learning to write: the second before I took thy mother, (when) I saw a terrible vision. And regarding them I prayed to the Lord. 3. I had laid me down in the house of my grandfather Mahalalel, (when) I saw in a vision how the heaven collapsed and was borne off and fell to the earth. 4. And when it fell to the earth I saw how the earth was swallowed up in a great abyss, and mountains were suspended on mountains, and hills sank down on hills, and high trees were rent from their stems, and hurled down and sunk in the abyss. 5. And thereupon a word fell into my mouth, and I lifted up (my voice) to cry aloud, and said: 'The earth is destroyed.' 6. And my grandfather Mahalalel waked me as I lay near him, and said unto me: 'Why dost thou cry so, my son, and why dost thou make such lamentation?' 7. And I recounted to him the whole vision which I had seen, and he said unto me: 'A terrible thing hast thou seen, my son, and of grave moment is thy dream-vision as to the secrets of all the sin of the earth: it must sink into the abyss and be destroyed with a great destruction. 8. And now, my son, arise and make petition to the Lord of

glory, since thou art a believer, that a remnant may remain on the earth, and that He may not destroy the whole earth. 9. My son, from heaven all this will come upon the earth, and upon the earth there will be great destruction. 10. After that I arose and prayed and implored and besought, and wrote down my prayer for the generations of the world, and I will show everything to thee, my son Methuselah. 11. And when I had gone forth below and seen the heaven, and the sun rising in the east, and the moon setting in the west, and a few stars, and the whole earth, and everything as †He had known† it in the beginning, then I blessed the Lord of judgement and extolled Him because He had made the sun to go forth from the windows of the east, †and he ascended and rose on the face of the heaven, and set out and kept traversing the path shown unto him.

CHAPTER LXXXIV.

1. And I lifted up my hands in righteousness and blessed the Holy and Great One, and spake with the breath of my mouth, and with the tongue of flesh, which God has made for the children of the flesh of men, that they should speak therewith, and He gave them breath and a tongue and a mouth that they should speak therewith:

2. 'Blessed be Thou, O Lord, King,

Great and mighty in Thy greatness, Lord of the whole creation of the heaven, King of kings and God of the whole world.

And Thy power and kingship and greatness abide for ever and ever,

And throughout all generations Thy dominion;

And all the heavens are Thy throne for ever,

And the whole earth Thy footstool for ever and ever.

3. For Thou hast made and Thou rulest all things,

And nothing is too hard for Thee,

Wisdom departs not **from the place of Thy throne, Nor turns away** from Thy presence.

And Thou knowest and seest and hearest everything,

And there is nothing hidden from Thee [for Thou seest everything].

4. And now the angels of Thy heavens are guilty of trespass,

And upon the flesh of men abideth Thy wrath until the great day of judgement.

5. And now, O God and Lord and Great King,

I implore and beseech Thee to fulfil my prayer,

To leave me a posterity on earth,

And not destroy all the flesh of man,

And make the earth without inhabitant,

So that there should be an eternal destruction.

6. And now, my Lord, destroy from the earth the flesh which has aroused Thy wrath,

But the flesh of righteousness and uprightness establish as a plant of the eternal seed, And hide not Thy face from the prayer of Thy servant, O Lord.'

CHAPTER LXXXV.

1. And after this I saw another dream, and I will show the whole dream to thee, my son. 2. And Enoch lifted up (his voice) and spake to his son Methuselah: 'To thee, my son, will I speak: hear my words--incline thine ear to the dream-vision of thy father. 3. Before I took thy mother Edna, I saw in a vision on my bed, and behold a bull came forth from the earth, and that bull was white; and after it came forth a heifer, and along with

this (latter) came forth two bulls, one of them black and the other red. 4. And that black bull gored the red one and pursued him over the earth, and thereupon I could no longer see that red bull. 5. But that black bull grew and that heifer went with him, and I saw that many oxen proceeded from him which resembled and followed him. 6. And that cow, that first one, went from the presence of that first bull in order to seek that red one, but found him not, and lamented with a great lamentation over him and sought him. 7. And I looked till that first bull came to her and quieted her, and from that time onward she cried no more. 8. And after that she bore another white bull, and after him she bore many bulls and black cows.

9. And I saw in my sleep that white bull likewise grow and become a great white bull, and from Him proceeded many white bulls, and they resembled him. And they began to beget many white bulls, which resembled them, one following the other, (even) many.

CHAPTER LXXXVI.

1. And again I saw with mine eyes as I slept, and I saw the heaven above, and behold a star fell from heaven, and it arose and eat and pastured amongst those oxen. 2. And after that I saw the large and the black oxen, and behold they all changed their stalls and pastures and their cattle, and began to live with each other. 3. And again I saw in the vision, and looked towards the heaven, and behold I saw many stars descend and cast themselves down from heaven to that first star, and they became bulls amongst those cattle and pastured with them [amongst them]. 4. And I looked at them and saw, and behold they all let out their privy members, like horses, and began to cover the cows of the oxen, and they all became pregnant and bare elephants, camels, and asses. 5. And all the oxen feared them and were affrighted at them, and began to bite with their teeth and to devour, and to gore with their horns. 6. And they began,

moreover, to devour those oxen; and behold all the children of the earth began to tremble and quake before them and to flee from them.

CHAPTER LXXXVII.

1. And again I saw how they began to gore each other and to devour each other, and the earth began to cry aloud. 2. And I raised mine eyes again to heaven, and I saw in the vision, and behold there came forth from heaven beings who were like white men: and four went forth from that place and three with them. 3. And those three that had last come forth grasped me by my hand and took me up, away from the generations of the earth, and raised me up to a lofty place, and showed me a tower raised high above the earth, and all the hills were lower.

4. And one said unto me: 'Remain here till thou seest everything that befalls those elephants, camels, and asses, and the stars and the oxen, and all of them.'

CHAPTER LXXXVIII.

1. And I saw one of those four who had come forth first, and he seized that first star which had fallen from the heaven, and bound it hand and foot and cast it into an abyss: now that abyss was narrow and deep, and horrible and dark. 2. And one of them drew a sword, and gave it to those elephants and camels and asses: then they began to smite each other, and the whole earth quaked because of them. 3. And as I was beholding in the vision, lo, one of those four who had come forth stoned (them) from heaven, and gathered and took all the great stars whose privy members were like those of horses, and bound them all hand and foot, and cast them in an abyss of the earth.

CHAPTER LXXXIX.

1. And one of those four went to that white bull and instructed him in a secret, without his being terrified: he was born a bull and became a man, and built for himself a great vessel and dwelt thereon; and three bulls dwelt with him in that vessel and they were covered in. 2. And again I raised mine eyes towards heaven and saw a lofty roof, with seven water torrents thereon, and those torrents flowed with much water into an enclosure. 3. And I saw again, and behold fountains were opened on the surface of that great enclosure, and that water began to swell and rise upon the surface, and I saw that enclosure till all its surface was covered with water. 4. And the water, the darkness, and mist increased upon it; and as I looked at the height of that water, that water had risen above the height of that enclosure, and was streaming over that enclosure, and it stood upon the earth. 5. And all the cattle of that enclosure were gathered together until I saw how they sank and were swallowed up and perished in that water. 6. But that vessel floated on the water, while all the oxen and elephants and camels and asses sank to the bottom with all the animals, so that I could no longer see them, and they were not able to escape, (but) perished and sank into the depths. 7. And again I saw in the vision till those water torrents were removed from that high roof, and the chasms of the earth were levelled up and other abysses were opened. 8. Then the water began to run down into these, till the earth became visible; but that vessel settled on the earth, and the darkness retired and light appeared. 9. But that white bull which had become a man came out of that vessel, and the three bulls with him, and one of those three was white like that bull, and one of them was red as blood, and one black: and that white bull departed from them.

10. And they began to bring forth beasts of the field and birds, so that there arose different genera: lions, tigers, wolves, dogs, hyenas, wild boars, foxes, squirrels, swine, falcons, vultures, kites, eagles, and ravens;

and among them was born a white bull. 11. And they began to bite one another; but that white bull which was born amongst them begat a wild ass and a white bull with it, and the wild asses multiplied. 12. But that bull which was born from him begat a black wild boar and a white sheep; and the former begat many boars, but that sheep begat twelve sheep. 13. And when those twelve sheep had grown, they gave up one of them to the asses, and those asses again gave up that sheep to the wolves, and that sheep grew up among the wolves. 14. And the Lord brought the eleven sheep to live with it and to pasture with it among the wolves: and they multiplied and became many flocks of sheep. 15. And the wolves began to fear them, and they oppressed them until they destroyed their little ones, and they cast their young into a river of much water: but those sheep began to cry aloud on account of their little ones, and to complain unto their Lord. 16. And a sheep which had been saved from the wolves fled and escaped to the wild asses; and I saw the sheep how they lamented and cried, and besought their Lord with all their might, till that Lord of the sheep descended at the voice of the sheep from a lofty abode, and came to them and pastured them.

17. And He called that sheep which had escaped the wolves, and spake with it concerning the wolves that it should admonish them not to touch the sheep. 18. And the sheep went to the wolves according to the word of the Lord, and another sheep met it and went with it, and the two went and entered together into the assembly of those wolves, and spake with them and admonished them not to touch the sheep from henceforth. 19. And thereupon I saw the wolves, and how they oppressed the sheep exceedingly with all their power; and the sheep cried aloud. 20. And the Lord came to the sheep and they began to smite those wolves: and the wolves began to make lamentation; but the sheep became quiet and forthwith ceased to cry out. 21. And I saw the sheep till they departed from amongst the wolves; but the eyes of the wolves were blinded, and those wolves departed in pursuit of the sheep with all their power. 22.

And the Lord of the sheep went with them, as their leader, and all His sheep followed Him: and his face was dazzling and glorious and terrible to behold. 23. But the wolves began to pursue those sheep till they reached a sea of water. 24. And that sea was divided, and the water stood on this side and on that before their face, and their Lord led them and placed Himself between them and the wolves. 25. And as those wolves did not yet see the sheep, they proceeded into the midst of that sea, and the wolves followed the sheep, and [those wolves] ran after them into that sea. 26. And when they saw the Lord of the sheep, they turned to flee before His face, but that sea gathered itself together, and became as it had been created, and the water swelled and rose till it covered those wolves. 27. And I saw till all the wolves who pursued those sheep perished and were drowned.

28. But the sheep escaped from that water and went forth into a wilderness, where there was no water and no grass; and they began to open their eyes and to see; and I saw the Lord of the sheep pasturing them and giving them water and grass, and that sheep going and leading them. 29. And that sheep ascended to the summit of that lofty rock, and the Lord of the sheep sent it to them. 30. And after that I saw the Lord of the sheep who stood before them, and His appearance was great and terrible and majestic, and all those sheep saw Him and were afraid before His face. 31. And they all feared and trembled because of Him, and they cried to that sheep with them [which was amongst them]: "We are not able to stand before our Lord or to behold Him." 32. And that sheep which led them again ascended to the summit of that rock, but the sheep began to be blinded and to wander from the way which he had showed them, but that sheep wot not thereof. 33. And the Lord of the sheep was wrathful exceedingly against them, and that sheep discovered it, and went down from the summit of the rock, and came to the sheep, and found the greatest part of them blinded and fallen away. 34. And when they saw it they feared and trembled at its presence, and desired to

return to their folds. 35. And that sheep took other sheep with it, and came to those sheep which had fallen away, and began to slay them; and the sheep feared its presence, and thus that sheep brought back those sheep that had fallen away, and they returned to their folds. 36. And I saw in this vision till that sheep became a man and built a house for the Lord of the sheep, and placed all the sheep in that house. 37. And I saw till this sheep which had met that sheep which led them fell asleep: and I saw till all the great sheep perished and little ones arose in their place, and they came to a pasture, and approached a stream of water. 38. Then that sheep, their leader which had become a man, withdrew from them and fell asleep, and all the sheep sought it and cried over it with a great crying. 39. And I saw till they left off crying for that sheep and crossed that stream of water, and there arose the two sheep as leaders in the place of those which had led them and fallen asleep (lit. "had fallen asleep and led them"). 40. And I saw till the sheep came to a goodly place, and a pleasant and glorious land, and I saw till those sheep were satisfied; and that house stood amongst them in the pleasant land.

41. And sometimes their eyes were opened, and sometimes blinded, till another sheep arose and led them and brought them all back, and their eyes were opened.

42. And the dogs and the foxes and the wild boars began to devour those sheep till the Lord of the sheep raised up [another sheep] a ram from their midst, which led them. 43. And that ram began to butt on either side those dogs, foxes, and wild boars till he had destroyed them †all†. 44. And that sheep whose eyes were opened saw that ram, which was amongst the sheep, **till**it †forsook its glory† and began to butt those sheep, and trampled upon them, and behaved itself unseemly. 45. And the Lord of the sheep sent the **lamb** to another **lamb** and raised it to being a ram and leader of the sheep instead of that ram which had †forsaken its glory†. 46. And it went to it and spake to it alone, and raised it to being a ram, and made it the prince and leader of the sheep; but during all these things those dogs oppressed the sheep. 47. And the first ram pursued that second ram, and that second ram arose and fled before

it; and I saw till those dogs pulled down the first ram. 48. And that second ram arose and led the [little] sheep. 49. And those sheep grew and multiplied; but all the dogs, and foxes, and wild boars feared and fled before it, and that ram butted and killed the wild beasts, and those wild beasts had no longer any power among the sheep and robbed them no more of ought. 48[b]. And that ram begat many sheep and fell asleep; and a little sheep became ram in its stead, and became prince and leader of those sheep.

50. And that house became great and broad, and it was built for those sheep: (and) a tower lofty and great was built on the house for the Lord of the sheep, and that house was low, but the tower was elevated and lofty, and the Lord of the sheep stood on that tower and they offered a full table before Him.

51. And again I saw those sheep that they again erred and went many ways, and forsook that their house, and the Lord of the sheep called some from amongst the sheep and sent them to the sheep, but the sheep began to slay them. 52. And one of them was saved and was not slain, and it sped away and cried aloud over the sheep; and they sought to slay it, but the Lord of the sheep saved it from the sheep, and brought it up to me, and caused it to dwell there. 53.

And many other sheep He sent to those sheep to testify unto them and lament over them. 54. And after that I saw that when they forsook the house of the Lord and His tower they fell away entirely, and their eyes were blinded; and I saw the Lord of the sheep how He wrought much slaughter amongst them in their herds until those sheep invited that slaughter and betrayed His place. 55. And He gave them over into the hands of the lions and tigers, and wolves and hyenas, and into the hand of the foxes, and to all the wild beasts, and those wild beasts began to tear in pieces those sheep. 56. And I saw that He forsook that their house and their tower and gave them all into the hand of the lions, to tear and devour them, into the hand of all the wild beasts. 57. And I began to cry aloud with all my power, and to appeal to the Lord of the sheep, and to represent to Him in regard to the sheep that they were devoured by all the wild beasts. 58. But He remained unmoved, though He saw it, and rejoiced that they were devoured and swallowed and robbed, and left them to be devoured in the hand of all the beasts. 59. And He called seventy shepherds, and cast those sheep to them that they might pasture them, and He spake to the shepherds and their companions: "Let each individual of you pasture the sheep henceforward, and everything that I shall command you that do ye. 60. And I will deliver them over unto you duly numbered, and tell you which of them are to be destroyed--and them destroy ye." And He gave over unto them those sheep. 61. And He called another and spake unto him: "Observe and mark everything that the shepherds will do to those sheep; for they will destroy more of them than I have commanded them. 62. And every excess and the destruction which will be wrought through the shepherds, record (namely) how many they destroy according to my command, and how many according to their own caprice: record against every individual shepherd all the destruction he effects.

63. And read out before me by number how many they destroy, and how many they deliver over for destruction, that I may have this as a testimony against them, and know every deed of the shepherds, that I may **comprehend** and see what they do, whether or not they abide by my command which I have commanded them. 64. But they shall not know it, and thou shalt not declare it to them, nor admonish them, but only record against each individual all the destruction which the shepherds effect each in his time and lay it all before me." 65. And I saw till those shepherds pastured in their season, and they began to slay and to destroy more than they were bidden, and they delivered those sheep into the hand of the lions. 66. And the lions and tigers eat and devoured the greater part of those sheep, and the wild boars eat along with them; and they burnt that tower and demolished that house. 67. And I became exceedingly sorrowful over that tower because that house of the sheep

was demolished, and afterwards I was unable to see if those sheep entered that house.

68. And the shepherds and their associates delivered over those sheep to all the wild beasts, to devour them, and each one of them received in his time a definite number: it was written by the other in a book how many each one of them destroyed of them. 69. And each one slew and destroyed many more than was prescribed; and I began to weep and lament on account of those sheep. 70. And thus in the vision I saw that one who wrote, how he wrote down every one that was destroyed by those shepherds, day by day, and carried up and laid down and showed actually the whole book to the Lord of the sheep--(even) everything that they had done, and all that each one of them had made away with, and all that they had given over to destruction. 71. And the book was read before the Lord of the sheep, and He took the book from his hand and read it and sealed it and laid it down.

72. And forthwith I saw how the shepherds pastured for twelve hours, and behold three of those sheep turned back and came and entered and began to build up all that had fallen down of that house; but the wild boars tried to hinder them, but they were not able. 73. And they began again to build as before, and they reared up that tower, and it was named the high tower; and they began again to place a table before the tower, but all the bread on it was polluted and not pure. 74. And as touching all this the eyes of those sheep were blinded so that they saw not, and (the eyes of) their shepherds likewise; and they delivered them in large numbers to their shepherds for destruction, and they trampled the sheep with their feet and devoured them. 75. And the Lord of the sheep remained unmoved till all the sheep were dispersed over the field and mingled with them (*i.e.* the beasts), and they (*i.e.* the shepherds) did not save them out of the hand of the beasts. 76. And this one who wrote the book carried it up, and showed it and read it before the Lord of the sheep,

and implored Him on their account, and besought Him on their account as he showed Him all the doings of the shepherds, and gave testimony before Him against all the shepherds. And he took the actual book and laid it down beside Him and departed.

CHAPTER XC.

1. And I saw till that in this manner thirty-five shepherds undertook the pasturing (of the sheep), and they severally completed their periods as did the first; and others received them into their hands, to pasture them for their period, each shepherd in his own period. 2. And after that I saw in my vision all the birds of heaven coming, the eagles, the vultures, the kites, the ravens; but the eagles led all the birds; and they began to devour those sheep, and to pick out their eyes and to devour their flesh. 3. And the sheep cried out because their flesh was being devoured by the birds, and as for me I looked and lamented in my sleep over that shepherd who pastured the sheep. 4. And I saw until those sheep were devoured by the dogs and eagles and kites, and they left neither flesh nor skin nor sinew remaining on them till only their bones stood there: and their bones too fell to the earth and the sheep became few. 5. And I saw until that twenty-three had undertaken the pasturing and completed in their several periods fifty-eight times.

6. But behold lambs were borne by those white sheep, and they began to open their eyes and to see, and to cry to the sheep. 7. Yea, they cried to them, but they did not hearken to what they said to them, but were exceedingly deaf, and their eyes were very exceedingly blinded. 8. And I saw in the vision how the ravens flew upon those lambs and took one of those lambs, and dashed the sheep in pieces and devoured them. 9. And I saw till horns grew upon those lambs, and the ravens cast down their horns; and I saw till there sprouted a great horn of one of those sheep, and their eyes were opened. 10. And it †looked at† them [and their eyes

opened], and it cried to the sheep, and the rams saw it and all ran to it. 11. And notwithstanding all this those eagles and vultures and ravens and kites still kept tearing the sheep and swooping down upon them and devouring them: still the sheep remained silent, but the rams lamented and cried out. 12. And those ravens fought and battled with it and sought to lay low its horn, but they had no power over it.

13. And I saw till the †shepherds and† eagles and those vultures and kites came, and †they cried to the ravens† that they should break the horn of that ram, and they battled and fought with it, and it battled with them and cried that its help might come.

14. And I saw till that man, who wrote down the names of the shepherds [and] carried up into the presence of the Lord of the sheep [came and helped it and showed it everything: he had come down for the help of that ram].

15. And I saw till the Lord of the sheep came unto them in wrath, and all who saw Him fled, and they all fell †into His shadow† from before His face.

16. All the eagles and vultures and ravens and kites were gathered together, and there came with them all the sheep of the field, yea, they all came together, and helped each other to break that horn of the ram.

17. And I saw that man, who wrote the book according to the command of the Lord, till he opened that book concerning the destruction which those twelve last shepherds had wrought, and showed that they had destroyed much more than their predecessors, before the Lord of the sheep.

18. And I saw till the Lord of the sheep came unto them and took in His hand the staff of His wrath, and smote the earth, and the earth clave asunder, and all the beasts and all the birds of the heaven fell from among those sheep, and were swallowed up in the earth and it covered them.

19. And I saw till a great sword was given to the sheep, and the sheep proceeded against all the beasts of the field to slay them, and all the beasts and the birds of the heaven fled before their face.

20. And I saw till a throne was erected in the pleasant land, and the Lord of the sheep sat

Himself thereon, and **the other** took the sealed books and opened those books before the Lord of the sheep. 21. And the Lord called those men the seven first white ones, and commanded that they should bring before Him, beginning with the first star which led the way, **all the** stars whose privy members were like those of horses, and they brought them all before Him. 22. And He said to that man who wrote before Him, being one of those seven white ones, and said unto him: "Take those seventy shepherds to whom I delivered the sheep, and who taking them on their own authority slew more than I commanded them." 23. And behold they were all bound, I saw, and they all stood before Him. 24. And the judgement was held first over the stars, and they were judged and found guilty, and went to the place of condemnation, and they were cast into an abyss, full of fire and flaming, and full of pillars of fire. 25. And those seventy shepherds were judged and found guilty, and they were cast into that fiery abyss. 26. And I saw at that time how a like abyss was opened in the midst of the earth, full of fire, and they brought those blinded sheep, and they were all judged and found guilty and cast into this fiery abyss, and they burned; now this abyss was to the right of that house. 27. And I saw those sheep burning †and their bones burning†.

28. And I stood up to see till they folded up that old house; and carried off all the pillars, and all the beams and ornaments of the house were at the same time folded up with it, and they carried it off and laid it in a place in the south of the land. 29. And I saw till the Lord of the sheep brought a new house greater and loftier than that first, and set it up in the place of the first which had beer folded up: all its pillars were new, and its

ornaments were new and larger than those of the first, the old one which He had taken away, and all the sheep were within it.

30. And I saw all the sheep which had been left, and all the beasts on the earth, and all the birds of the heaven, falling down and doing homage to those sheep and making petition to and obeying them in every **thing**. 31. And thereafter those three who were clothed in white and had seized me by my hand [who had taken me up before], and the hand of that ram also seizing hold of me, they took me up and set me down in the midst of those sheep before the judgement took place†. 32. And those sheep were all white, and their wool was abundant and clean. 33. And all that had been destroyed and dispersed, and all the beasts of the field, and all the birds of the heaven, assembled in that house, and the Lord of the sheep rejoiced with great joy because they were all good and had returned to His house. 34. And I saw till they laid down that sword, which had been given to the sheep, and they brought it back into the house, and it was sealed before the presence of the Lord, and all the sheep were invited into that house, but it held them not. 35. And the eyes of them all were opened, and they saw the good, and there was not one among them that did not see. 36. And I saw that that house was large and broad and very full.

37. And I saw that a white bull was born, with large horns and all the beasts of the field and all the birds of the air feared him and made petition to him all the time. 38. And I saw till all their generations were transformed, and they all became white bulls; and the first among them became a **lamb**, and that **lamb** became a great animal and had great black horns on its head; and the Lord of the sheep rejoiced over **it** and over all the oxen. 39. And I slept in their midst: and I awoke and saw everything. 40. This is the vision which I saw while I slept, and I awoke and blessed the Lord of righteousness and gave Him glory. 41. Then I wept with a great weeping and my tears stayed not till I could no longer endure it:

when I saw, they flowed on account of what I had seen; for everything shall come and be fulfilled, and all the deeds of men in their order were shown to me. 42. On that night I remembered the first dream, and because of it I wept and was troubled--because I had seen that vision.'

The Concluding Section Of The Book

CHAPTER XCI.

1. The book written by Enoch--[Enoch indeed wrote this complete doctrine of wisdom, (which is) praised of all men and a judge of all the earth] for all my children who shall dwell on the earth. And for the future generations who shall observe uprightness and peace.

2. Let not your spirit be troubled on account of the times; For the Holy and Great One has appointed days for all things.

3. And the righteous one shall arise from sleep,

[Shall arise] and walk in the paths of righteousness,

And all his path and conversation shall be in eternal goodness and grace.

4. He will be gracious to the righteous and give him eternal uprightness,

And He will give him power so that he shall be (endowed) with goodness and righteousness. And he shall walk in eternal light.

5. And sin shall perish in darkness for ever,

And shall no more be seen from that day for evermore.

CHAPTER XCII.

1. 'And now, my son Methuselah, call to me all thy brothers

And gather together to me all the sons of thy mother;

For the word calls me,

And the spirit is poured out upon me,

That I may show you everything That shall befall you for ever.'

2 And there upon Methuselah went and summoned to him all his brothers and assembled his relatives. 3 And he spake unto all the children of righteousness and said:

'Hear, ye sons of Enoch, all the words of your father, And hearken aright to the voice of my mouth; For I exhort you and say unto you, beloved:

Love uprightness and walk therein.

4. And draw not nigh to uprightness with a double heart, And associate not with those of a double heart, But walk in righteousness, my sons.

And it shall guide you on good paths,

And righteousness shall be your companion.

5. For I know that violence **must** increase on the earth, And a great chastisement be executed on the earth, And all unrighteousness come to an end:

Yea, it shall be cut off from its roots, And its whole structure be destroyed.

6. And unrighteousness shall again be consummated on the earth, And all the deeds of unrighteousness and of violence And transgression shall prevail in a twofold degree.

7. And when sin and unrighteousness and blasphemy

And violence in all kinds of deeds increase,

And apostasy and transgression and uncleanness increase,

A great chastisement shall come from heaven upon all these, And the holy Lord will come forth with wrath and chastisement To execute judgement on earth.

8. In those days violence shall be cut off from its roots, And the roots of unrighteousness together with deceit, And they shall be destroyed from under heaven.

9. And all the idols of the heathen shall be abandoned,

And the temples burned with fire,

And they shall remove them from the whole earth,

And they (*i.e.* the heathen) shall be cast into the judgement of fire, And shall perish in wrath and in grievous judgement for ever.

10. And the righteous shall arise from their sleep, And wisdom shall arise and be given unto them.

[11. And after that the roots of unrighteousness shall be cut off, and the sinners shall be destroyed by the sword . . . shall be cut off from the blasphemers in every place, and those who plan violence and those who commit blasphemy shall perish by the sword.]

18. And now I tell you, my sons, and show you The paths of righteousness and the paths of violence. Yea, I will show them to you again

That ye may know what will come to pass.

19. And now, hearken unto me, my sons,

And walk in the paths of righteousness,

And walk not in the paths of violence;

For all who walk in the paths of unrighteousness shall perish for ever.'

CHAPTER XCIII.

1. And after that Enoch both †gave† and began to recount from the books. And Enoch said:

'Concerning the children of righteousness and concerning the elect of the world, And concerning the plant of uprightness, I will speak these things, Yea, I Enoch will declare (them) unto you, my sons:

According to that which appeared to me in the heavenly vision,

And which I have known through the word of the holy angels, And have learnt from the heavenly tablets.'

3. And Enoch began to recount from the books and said:
'I was born the seventh in the first week,

While judgement and righteousness still endured.

4. And after me there shall arise in the second week great wickedness, And deceit shall have sprung up; And in it there shall be the first end.

And in it a man shall be saved;

And after it is ended unrighteousness shall grow up, And a law shall be made for the sinners.

5. And after that in the third week at its close

A man shall be elected as the plant of righteous judgement,

And **his posterity** shall become the plant of righteousness for evermore.

6. And after that in the fourth week, at its close,

Visions of the holy and righteous shall be seen,

And a law for all generations and an enclosure shall be made for them.

7. And after that in the fifth week, at its close,

The house of glory and dominion shall be built for ever.

8. And after that in the sixth week all who live in it shall be blinded,
And the hearts of all of them shall godlessly forsake wisdom.

And in it a man shall ascend;

And at its close the house of dominion shall be burnt with fire, And the whole race of the chosen root shall be dispersed.

9. And after that in the seventh week shall an apostate generation arise,
And many shall be its deeds, And all its deeds shall be apostate.

10. And at its close shall be elected

The elect righteous of the eternal plant of righteousness, To receive sevenfold instruction concerning all His creation.

[11. For who is there of all the children of men that is able to hear the voice of the Holy One without being troubled? And who can think His thoughts? and who is there that can behold all the works of heaven? 12. And how should there be one who could behold the heaven, and who is there that could understand the things of heaven and see a soul or a spirit and could tell thereof, or ascend and see all their ends and think them or do like them? 13. And who is there of all men that could know what is the breadth and the length of the earth, and to whom has been shown the measure of all of them? 14. Or is there any one who could discern the length of the heaven and how great is its height, and upon what it is founded, and how great is the number of the stars, and where all the luminaries rest?]

12. And after that there shall be another, the eighth week, that of righteousness, And a sword shall be given to it that a righteous judgement may be executed on the oppressors,

And sinners shall be delivered into the hands of the righteous.

13 And at its close they shall acquire houses through their righteousness, And a house shall be built for the Great King in glory for evermore, 14*d*. And all mankind shall look to the path of uprightness.

14*a*. And after that, in the ninth week, the righteous judgement shall be revealed to the whole world,

b. And all the works of the godless shall vanish from all the earth,

c. And the world shall be written down for destruction.

15. And after this, in the tenth week in the seventh part,

There shall be the great eternal judgement,

In which He will execute vengeance amongst the angels.

16. And the first heaven shall depart and pass away,

And a new heaven shall appear,

And all the powers of the heavens shall give sevenfold light.

17. And after that there will be many weeks without number for ever, And all shall be in goodness and righteousness, And sin shall no more be mentioned for ever.

CHAPTER XCIV.

1. And now I say unto you, my sons, love righteousness and walk therein;

For the paths of righteousness are worthy of acceptation,

But the paths of unrighteousness shall suddenly be destroyed and vanish.

2. And to certain men of a generation shall the paths of violence and of death be revealed, And they shall hold themselves afar from them, And shall not follow them.

3. And now I say unto you the righteous:

Walk not in the paths of wickedness, nor in the paths of death, And draw not nigh to them, lest ye be destroyed.

4. But seek and choose for yourselves righteousness and an elect life, And walk in the paths of peace, And ye shall live and prosper.

5. And hold fast my words in the thoughts of your hearts, And suffer them not to be effaced from your hearts;

For I know that sinners will tempt men to **evilly-entreat** wisdom, So that no place may be found for her, And no manner of temptation may minish.

6. Woe to those who build unrighteousness and oppression

And lay deceit as a foundation;

For they shall be suddenly overthrown, And they shall have no peace.

7. Woe to those who build their houses with sin; For from all their foundations shall they be overthrown, And by the sword shall they fall.

[And those who acquire gold and silver in judgement suddenly shall perish.]

8. Woe to you, ye rich, for ye have trusted in your riches,

And from your riches shall ye depart,

Because ye have not remembered the Most High in the days of your riches.

9. Ye have committed blasphemy and unrighteousness,

And have become ready for the day of slaughter, And the day of darkness and the day of the great judgement.

10. Thus I speak and declare unto you:

He who hath created you will overthrow you, And for your fall there shall be no compassion, And your Creator will rejoice at your destruction.

11. And your righteous ones in those days shall be A reproach to the sinners and the godless.

CHAPTER XCV.

1. Oh that mine eyes were [a cloud of] waters

That I might weep over you,

And pour down my tears as a cloud †of† waters: That so I might rest from my trouble of heart!

2. †Who has permitted you to practice reproaches and wickedness? And so judgement shall overtake you, sinners. †

3. Fear not the sinners, ye righteous;

For again will the Lord deliver them into your hands,

That ye may execute judgement upon them according to your desires.

4. Woe to you who fulminate anathemas which cannot be reversed: Healing shall therefore be far from you because of your sins.

5. Woe to you who requite your neighbour with evil; For ye shall be requited according to your works.

6. Woe to you, lying witnesses, And to those who weigh out injustice, For suddenly shall ye perish.

7. Woe to you, sinners, for ye persecute the righteous; For ye shall be delivered up and persecuted because of injustice, And heavy shall its yoke be upon you.

CHAPTER XCVI.

1. Be hopeful, ye righteous; for suddenly shall the sinners perish before you, And ye shall have lordship over them according to your desires.

[2. And in the day of the tribulation of the sinners,

Your children shall mount and rise as eagles,

And higher than the vultures will be your nest,

And ye shall ascend and enter the crevices of the earth,

And the clefts of the rock for ever as coneys before the unrighteous, And the sirens shall sigh because of you-and weep.]

3. Wherefore fear not, ye that have suffered;

For healing shall be your portion,

And a bright light shall enlighten you,

And the voice of rest ye shall hear from heaven.

4. Woe unto you, ye sinners, for your riches make you appear like the righteous,

But your hearts convict you of being sinners,

And this fact shall be a testimony against you for a memorial of (your) evil deeds.

5. Woe to you who devour the finest of the wheat,

And drink **wine in large bowls**,

And tread under foot the lowly with your might.

6. Woe to you who drink water **from every fountain**, For suddenly shall ye be consumed and wither away, Because ye have forsaken the fountain of life.

7. Woe to you who work unrighteousness And deceit and blasphemy:

It shall be a memorial against you for evil.

8. Woe to you, ye mighty,

Who with might oppress the righteous;

For the day of your destruction is coming.

In those days many and good days shall come to the righteous--in the day of your judgement.

CHAPTER XCVII.

1. Believe, ye righteous, that the sinners will become a shame And perish in the day of unrighteousness.

2. Be it known unto you (ye sinners) that the Most High is mindful of your destruction, And the angels of heaven rejoice over your destruction.

3. What will ye do, ye sinners,

And whither will ye flee on that day of judgement, When ye hear the voice of the prayer of the righteous?

4. Yea, ye shall fare like unto them,

Against whom this word shall be a testimony: "Ye have been companions of sinners."

5. And in those days the prayer of the righteous shall reach unto the Lord, And for you the days of your judgement shall come.

6. And all the words of your unrighteousness shall be read out before the Great Holy One,

And your faces shall be covered with shame,

And He will reject every work which is grounded on unrighteousness.

7. Woe to you, ye sinners, who live on the mid ocean and on the dry land, Whose remembrance is evil against you.

8. Woe to you who acquire silver and gold in unrighteousness and say: "We have become rich with riches and have possessions; And have acquired everything we have desired.

9. And now let us do what we purposed: For we have gathered silver,

9[d] And many are the husbandmen in our houses."

9[e] And our granaries are (brim) full as with water,

10 Yea and like water your lies shall flow away;

For your riches shall not abide But speedily ascend from you;

For ye have acquired it all in unrighteousness, And ye shall be given over to a great curse.

CHAPTER XCVIII.

1. And now I swear unto you, to the wise and to the foolish, For ye shall have manifold experiences on the earth.

2. For ye men shall put on more adornments than a woman, And coloured garments more than a virgin:

In royalty and in grandeur and in power,

And in silver and in gold and in purple,

And in splendour and in food they shall be poured out as water.

3. Therefore they shall be wanting in doctrine and wisdom,

And they shall perish thereby together with their possessions;

And with all their glory and their splendour,

And in shame and in slaughter and in great destitution, Their spirits shall be cast into the furnace of fire.

4. I have sworn unto you, ye sinners, as a mountain has not become a slave,

And a hill does not become the handmaid of a woman,

Even so sin has not been sent upon the earth,

But man of himself has created it,

And under a great curse shall they fall who commit it.

5. And barrenness has not been given to the woman,

But on account of the deeds of her own hands she dies without children.

6. I have sworn unto you, ye sinners, by the Holy Great One, That all your evil deeds are revealed in the heavens,

And that none of your deeds of oppression are covered and hidden.

7. And do not think in your spirit nor say in your heart that ye do not know and that ye do not see that every sin is every day recorded in heaven in the presence of the Most High. 8. From henceforth ye know that all your oppression wherewith ye oppress is written down every day till the day of your judgement.

9. Woe to you, ye fools, for through your folly shall ye perish: and ye transgress against the wise, and so good hap shall not be your portion. 10. And now, know ye that ye are prepared for the day of destruction: wherefore do not hope to live, ye sinners, but ye shall depart and die; for ye know no ransom; for ye are prepared for the day of the great judgement, for the day of tribulation and great shame for your spirits.

11. Woe to you, ye obstinate of heart, who work wickedness and eat blood:

Whence have ye good things to eat and to drink and to be filled? From all the good things which the Lord the Most High has placed in abundance on the earth; therefore ye shall have no peace. 12. Woe to you who love the deeds of unrighteousness: wherefore do ye hope for good hap unto yourselves? know that ye shall be delivered into the hands of the righteous, and they shall cut off your necks and slay you, and have no mercy upon you. 13. Woe to you who rejoice in the tribulation of the righteous; for no grave shall be dug for you. 14. Woe to you who set at nought the words of the righteous; for ye shall have no hope of life. 15. Woe to you who write down lying and godless words; for they write down their lies that men may hear them and act godlessly towards (their) neighbour. 16. Therefore they shall have no peace but die a sudden death.

CHAPTER XCIX.

1. Woe to you who work godlessness, And glory in lying and extol them:

Ye shall perish, and no happy life shall be yours.

2. Woe to them who pervert the words of uprightness,

And transgress the eternal law,

And transform themselves into what they were not [into sinners]: They shall be trodden under foot upon the earth.

3. In those days make ready, ye righteous, to raise your prayers as **a** memorial,

And place them as a testimony before the angels,

That they may place the sin of the sinners for a memorial before the Most High.

4. In those days the nations shall be stirred up,

And the families of the nations shall arise on the day of destruction.

5. And in those days the destitute shall go forth and carry off their children, And they shall abandon them, so that their children shall perish through them: Yea, they shall abandon their children (that are still) sucklings, and not return to them, And shall have no pity on their beloved ones.

6. And again I swear to you, ye sinners, that sin is prepared for a day of unceasing bloodshed. 7. And they who worship stones, and grave images of gold and silver and wood 〈and stone〉 and clay, and those who worship impure spirits and demons, and all kinds of idols not according to knowledge, shall get no manner of help from them.

8. And they shall become godless by reason of the folly of their hearts, And their eyes shall be blinded through the fear of their hearts And through visions in their dreams.

9. Through these they shall become godless and fearful; For they shall have wrought all their work in a lie, And shall have worshiped a stone:

Therefore in an instant shall they perish.

10. But in those days blessed are all they who accept the words of wisdom, and understand them,

And observe the paths of the Most High, and walk in the path of His righteousness, And become not godless with the godless; For they shall be saved.

11. Woe to you who spread evil to your neighbours; For you shall be

12. slain in Sheol.

13. Woe to you who make deceitful and false measures, And (to them) who cause bitterness on the earth; For they shall thereby be utterly consumed.

14. Woe to you who build your houses through the grievous toil of others, And all their building materials are the bricks and stones of sin; I tell you ye shall have no peace.

15. Woe to them who reject the measure and eternal heritage of their fathers And whose souls follow after idols; For they shall have no rest.

16. Woe to them who work unrighteousness and help oppression, And slay their neighbours until the day of the great judgement.

17. For He shall cast down your glory,

And bring affliction on your hearts,

And shall arouse **His fierce indignation**,

And destroy you all with the sword;

And all the holy and righteous shall remember your sins.

CHAPTER C.

1. And in those days in one place the fathers together with their sons shall be smitten And brothers one with another shall fall in death Till the streams flow with their blood.

2 .For a man shall not withhold his hand from slaying his sons and his sons' sons, And the sinner shall not withhold his hand from his honoured brother: From dawn till sunset they shall slay one another.

3. And the horse shall walk up to the breast in the blood of sinners, And the chariot shall be submerged to its height.

4 In those days the angels shall descend into the secret places

And gather together into one place all those who brought down sin And the Most High will arise on that day of judgement To execute great judgement amongst sinners.

5. And over all the righteous and holy He will appoint guardians from amongst the holy angels

To guard them as the apple of an eye,

Until He makes an end of all wickedness and all sin,

And though the righteous sleep a long sleep, they have nought to fear.

6. And (then) the children of the earth shall see the wise **in security**,

And shall understand all the words of this book,

And recognize that their riches shall not be able to save them In the overthrow of their sins.

7. Woe to you, Sinners, on the day of strong anguish, **Ye who afflict** the righteous and burn them with fire: Ye shall be requited according to your works.

8. Woe to you, ye obstinate of heart, Who watch in order to devise wickedness: Therefore shall fear come upon you And there shall be none to help you.

9. Woe to you, ye sinners, on account of the words of your mouth,

And on account of the deeds of your hands which your godlessness as wrought, In blazing flames burning worse than fire shall ye burn.

10 And now, know ye that from the angels He will inquire as to your deeds in heaven, from the sun and from the moon and from the stars in reference to your sins because upon the earth ye execute judgement on the righteous. 11. And He will summon to testify against you every cloud and mist and dew and rain; for they shall all be withheld because of you from descending upon you, and they shall be mindful of your sins. 12. And now give presents to the rain that it be not withheld from descending upon you, nor yet the dew, when it has received gold and silver from you that it may descend. 13. When the hoar-frost and snow with their chilliness, and all the snow-storms with all their plagues fall upon you, in those days ye shall not be able to stand before them.

CHAPTER CI.

1. Observe the heaven, ye children of heaven, and every work of the Most High, and fear ye Him and work no evil in His presence. 2. If He closes the windows of heaven, and withholds the rain and the dew from descending on the earth on your account, what will ye do then? 3. And if He sends His anger upon you because of your deeds, ye cannot petition Him; for ye spake proud and insolent words against His righteousness: therefore ye shall have no peace.

4. And see ye not the **sailors** of the ships, how their ships are tossed to and fro by the waves, and are shaken by the winds, and are in sore trouble? 5. And therefore do they fear because all their goodly possessions go upon the sea with them, and they have evil forebodings of heart that the sea will swallow them and they will perish therein.

6. Are not the entire sea and all its waters, and all its movements, the work of the Most High, and has He not set limits to its doings, and confined it throughout by the sand? 7. And at His reproof it is afraid and dries up, and all its fish die and all that is in it; But ye sinners that are on the earth fear Him not. 8. Has He not made the heaven and the earth, and all that is therein? Who has given understanding and wisdom to everything that moves on the earth and in the sea. 9. Do not the **sailors** of the ships fear the sea? Yet sinners fear not the Most High.

Chapter CII.

1. In those days when He hath brought a grievous fire upon you, Whither will ye flee, and where will ye find deliverance?

And when He launches forth His Word against you Will you not be affrighted and fear?

2. And all the luminaries shall be affrighted with great fear, And all the earth shall be affrighted and tremble and be alarmed.

3. And all the †angels shall execute their commands†

And shall seek to hide themselves from the presence of the Great Glory,

And the children of earth shall tremble and quake; And ye sinners shall be cursed for ever, And ye shall have no peace.

4. Fear ye not, ye souls of the righteous,

And be hopeful ye that have died in righteousness.

5. And grieve not if your soul into Sheol has descended in grief,

And that in your life your body fared not according to your goodness, But **wait for** the day of the **judgement** of sinners And for the day of cursing and chastisement.

6. And yet when ye die the sinners speak over you:

"As we die, so die the righteous,

And what benefit do they reap for their deeds?

7. Behold, even as we, so do they die in grief and darkness, And what have they more than we? From henceforth we are equal.

8. And what will they receive and what will they see for ever?

Behold, they too have died,

And henceforth for ever shall they see no light."

9. I tell you, ye sinners, ye are content to eat and drink, and rob and sin, and strip men naked, and acquire wealth and see good days.
10. Have ye seen the righteous how their end falls out, that no manner of violence is found in them till their death?

11. "Nevertheless they perished and became as though they had not been, and their spirits descended into Sheol in tribulation."

CHAPTER CIII.

1. Now, therefore, I swear to you, the righteous, by the glory of the Great and Honoured and 2 Mighty One in dominion, and by His greatness I swear to you:

2. I know a mystery

And have read the heavenly tablets,

And have seen the holy books,

And have found written therein and inscribed regarding them:

3. That all goodness and joy and glory are prepared for them,

And written down for the spirits of those who have died in righteousness, And that manifold good shall be given to you in recompense for your labours, And that your lot is abundantly beyond the lot of the living.

4. And the spirits of you who have died in righteousness shall live and rejoice,

And their spirits shall not perish, nor their memorial from before the face of the Great One Unto all the generations of the world: wherefore no longer fear their contumely.

5. Woe to you, ye sinners, when ye have died,

If ye die in the wealth of your sins,

And those who are like you say regarding you:

'Blessed are the sinners: they have seen all their days.

6. And how they have died in prosperity and in wealth,

And have not seen tribulation or murder in their life;

And they have died in honour,

And judgement has not been executed on them during their life."

7. Know ye, that their souls will be made to descend into Sheol And they shall be wretched in their great tribulation.

8. And into darkness and chains and a burning flame where there is grievous judgement shall your spirits enter;

And the great judgement shall be for all the generations of the world. Woe to you, for ye shall have no peace.

9. Say not in regard to the righteous and good who are in life:

"In our troubled days we have toiled laboriously and experienced every trouble, And met with much evil and been consumed, And have become few and our spirit small.

10. And we have been destroyed and have not found any to help us even with a word: We have been tortured [and destroyed], and not hoped to see life from day to day.

11. We hoped to be the head and have become the tail:

We have toiled laboriously and had no satisfaction in our toil; And we have become the food of the sinners and the unrighteous, And they have laid their yoke heavily upon us.

12. They have had dominion over us that hated us †and smote us; And to those that hated us† we have bowed our necks But they pitied us not.

13. We desired to get away from them that we might escape and be at rest, But found no place whereunto we should flee and be safe from them.

14. And are complained to the rulers in our tribulation,

And cried out against those who devoured us, But they did not attend to our cries And would not hearken to our voice.

15. And they helped those who robbed us and devoured us and those who made us few; and they concealed their oppression, and they did not remove from us the yoke of those that devoured us and dispersed us and murdered us, and they concealed their murder, and remembered not that they had lifted up their hands against us.

CHAPTER CIV.

1. I swear unto you, that in heaven the angels remember you for good before the glory of the Great One: and your names are written before the

glory of the Great One. 2. Be hopeful; for aforetime ye were put to shame through ill and affliction; but now ye shall shine as the lights of heaven, ye shall shine and ye shall be seen, and the portals of heaven shall be opened to you. 3. And in your cry, cry for judgement, and it shall appear to you; for all your tribulation shall be visited on the rulers, and on all who helped those who plundered you. 4. Be hopeful, and cast not away your hopes for ye shall have great joy as the angels of heaven. 5. What shall ye be obliged to do? Ye shall not have to hide on the day of the great judgement and ye shall not be found as sinners, and the eternal judgement shall be far from you for all the generations of the world. 6. And now fear not, ye righteous, when ye see the sinners growing strong and prospering in their ways: be not companions with them, but keep afar from their violence; for ye shall become companions of the hosts of heaven. 7. And, although ye sinners say: "All our sins shall not be searched out and be written down," nevertheless they shall write down all your sins every day. 8. And now I show unto you that light and darkness, day and night, see all your sins. 9. Be not godless in your hearts, and lie not and alter not the words of uprightness, nor charge with lying the words of the Holy Great One, nor take account of your idols; for all your lying and all your godlessness issue not in righteousness but in great sin. 10. And now I know this mystery, that sinners will alter and pervert the words of righteousness in many ways, and will speak wicked words, and lie, and practice great deceits, and write books concerning their words. 11. But when they write down truthfully all my words in their languages, and do not change or minish ought from my words but write them all down truthfully--all that I first testified concerning them. 12. Then, I know another mystery, that books will be given to the righteous and the wise to become a cause of joy and uprightness and much wisdom. 13. And to them shall the books be given, and they shall believe in them and rejoice over them, and then shall all the righteous who have learnt therefrom all the paths of uprightness be recompensed.'

CHAPTER CV.

1. In those days the Lord bade (them) to summon and testify to the children of earth concerning their wisdom: Show (it) unto them; for ye are their guides, and a recompense over the whole earth. 2. For I and My son will be united with them for ever in the paths of uprightness in their lives; and ye shall have peace: rejoice, ye children of uprightness. Amen.

Fragment Of The Book Of Noah

CHAPTER CVI.

1. And after some days my son Methuselah took a wife for his son Lamech, and she became pregnant by him and bore a son. 2. And his body was white as snow and red as the blooming of a rose, and the hair of his head †and his long locks were white as wool, and his eyes beautiful†. And when he opened his eyes, he lighted up the whole house like the sun, and the whole house was very bright. 3. And thereupon he arose in the hands of the midwife, opened his mouth, and †conversed with† the Lord of righteousness. 4. And his father Lamech was afraid of him and fled, and came to his father Methuselah. 5. And he said unto him: 'I have begotten a strange son, diverse from and unlike man, and resembling the sons of the God of heaven; and his nature is different and he is not like us, and his eyes are as the rays of the sun, and his countenance is glorious. 6. And it seems to me that he is not sprung from me but from the angels, and I fear that in his days a wonder may be wrought on the earth. 7. And now, my father, I am here to petition thee and implore thee that thou mayest go to Enoch, our father, and learn from him the truth, for his dwelling-place is amongst the angels.' 8. And when Methuselah heard the words of his son, he came to me to the ends of the earth; for he had heard that I was there, and he cried aloud, and I heard his voice and I came to him.

And 1 said unto him: 'Behold, here am I, my son, **wherefore** hast thou come to me?' 9. And he answered and said: 'Because of a great cause of anxiety have I come to thee, and because of a disturbing vision have I approached. 10. And now, my father, hear me: unto Lamech my son there hath been born a son, the like of whom there is none, and his nature is not like man's nature, and the colour of his body is whiter than snow and redder than the bloom of a rose, and the hair of his head is whiter than white wool, and his eyes are like the rays of the sun, and he opened his eyes and thereupon lighted up the whole house. 11. And he arose in the hands of the midwife, and opened his mouth and blessed the Lord of heaven. 12. And his father Lamech became afraid and fled to me, and did not believe that he was sprung from him, but that he was in the likeness of the angels of heaven; and behold I have come to thee that thou mayest make known to me the truth.' 13. And I, Enoch, answered and said unto him: 'The Lord will do a new thing on the earth, and this I have already seen in a vision, and make known to thee that in the generation of my father Jared some of the **angels** of heaven transgressed the word of the Lord. 14. And behold they commit sin and transgress the law, and have united themselves with women and commit sin with them, and have married some of them, and have begot children by them. 17. And they shall produce on the earth giants not according to the spirit, but according to the flesh, and there shall be a great punishment on the earth, and the earth shall be cleansed from all impurity. 15. Yea, there shall come a great destruction over the whole earth, and there shall be a deluge and a great destruction for one year. 16. And this son who has been born unto you shall be left on the earth, and his three children shall be saved with him: when all mankind that are on the earth shall die [he and his sons shall be saved]. 18. And now make known to thy son Lamech that he who has been born is in truth his son, and call his name Noah; for he shall be left to you, and he and his sons shall be saved from the destruction, which shall come upon the earth on account of all the sin and all the unrighteousness, which shall be consummated on the earth in his days. 19. And after that there shall be still more unrighteousness than that which was first consummated on the earth; for I know the mysteries of the holy ones; for He, the Lord, has showed me and informed me, and I have read (them) in the heavenly tablets.

CHAPTER CVII.

1. And I saw written on them that generation upon generation shall transgress, till a generation of righteousness arises, and transgression is destroyed and sin passes away from the earth, and all manner of good comes upon it. 2. And now, my son, go and make known to thy son Lamech that this son, which has been born, is in truth his son, and that (this) is no lie.' 3. And when Methuselah had heard the words of his father Enoch--for he had shown to him everything in secret--he returned and showed (them) to him and called the name of that son Noah; for he will comfort the earth after all the destruction.

THE END

An Appendix To The Book Of Enoch

CHAPTER CVIII.

1. Another book which Enoch wrote for his son Methuselah and for those who will come after him, and keep the law in the last days.

2. Ye who have done good shall wait for those days till an end is made of those who work evil; and an end of the might of the transgressors.

3. And wait ye indeed till sin has passed away, for their names shall be blotted out of the book of life and out of the holy books, and their seed shall be destroyed for ever, and their spirits shall be slain, and they shall cry and make lamentation in a place that is a chaotic wilderness, and **in the fire shall they burn**; for there is no earth there.

4. And I saw there something like an invisible cloud; for by reason of its depth I could not look over, and I saw a flame of fire blazing brightly, and things like shining mountains circling and sweeping to and fro.

5. And I asked one of the holy angels who was with me and said unto him: 'What is this shining thing? for it is not a heaven but only the flame of a blazing fire, and the voice of weeping and crying and lamentation and strong pain.'

6. And he said unto me: 'This place which thou seest--here are cast the spirits of sinners and blasphemers, and of those who work wickedness, and of those who pervert everything that the Lord hath spoken through the mouth of the prophets--(even) the things that shall be.

7. For some of them are written and inscribed above in the heaven, in order that the angels may read them and know that which shall befall the sinners, and the spirits of the humble, and of those who have afflicted their bodies, and been recompensed by God; and of those who have been put to shame by wicked men:

8. Who love God and loved neither gold nor silver nor any of the good things which are in the world, but gave over their bodies to torture.

9. Who, since they came into being, longed not after earthly food, but regarded everything as a passing breath, and lived accordingly, and the Lord tried them much, and their spirits were found pure so that they should bless His name.

10. And all the blessings destined for them I have recounted in the books. And he hath assigned them their recompense, because they have been found to be such as loved heaven more than their life in the world, and though they were trodden under foot of wicked men, and experienced abuse and reviling from them and were put to shame, yet they blessed Me.

11. And now I will summon the spirits of the good who belong to the generation of light, and I will transform those who were born in darkness, who in the flesh were not recompensed with such honour as their faithfulness deserved.

12. And I will bring forth in shining light those who have loved My holy name, and I will seat each on the throne of his honour.

13. And they shall be resplendent for times without number; for righteousness is the judgement of God; for to the faithful He will give faithfulness in the habitation of upright paths.

14. And they shall see those who were, born in darkness led into darkness, while the righteous shall be resplendent.

15. And the sinners shall cry aloud and see them resplendent, and they indeed will go where days and seasons are prescribed for them.'

Printed in Dunstable, United Kingdom

70659365R00100